THE BOOK OF STYLING

AN INSIDER'S GUIDE TO CREATING YOUR OWN LOOK

First published in 2012 by Zest Books
35 Stillman Street, Suite 121, San Francisco, CA 94107
www.zestbooks.net
Created and produced by Zest Books, San Francisco, CA

© 2012 by Zest Books LLC

Typeset in Sabon and Gill Sans

Teen Nonfiction / Clothing & Dress / Art & Fashion

Library of Congress Control Number: 2012934246

ISBN: 978-0-9827322-4-3

CREDITS
BOOK EDITOR: Daniel Harmon
CREATIVE DIRECTOR: Hallie Warshaw
ART DIRECTOR/COVER DESIGN: Tanya Napier
GRAPHIC DESIGN: Marissa Feind
MANAGING EDITOR: Pam McElroy
PRODUCTION EDITOR: Keith Snyder
RESEARCH EDITOR: Nikki Roddy
EDITORIAL ASSISTANT: Ann Edwards

Manufactured in China
SCP 10 9 8 7 6 5 4 3 2 1
4500361571

Every effort has been made to ensure that the information presented is accurate. The publisher disclaims any liability for injuries, losses, untoward results, or any other damages that may result from the use of the information in this book.

THE BOOK OF STYLING

AN INSIDER'S GUIDE TO CREATING YOUR OWN LOOK

Somer
Flaherty

From the Author

I've always loved style and fashion, but it took me a long time to realize that I could make styling my career. (I mean, journalism school taught me a lot about crime, technology, art, and local politics, but the newsroom isn't the best place to engage in the timeless debate over heels vs. flats.) But luckily, not long after I graduated, I got a job at a magazine where writing about fashion was accepted, encouraged, and even applauded. While I was there I was responsible for writing a monthly fashion trends column, overseeing the fashion credits printed in the magazine, pulling looks together for the photo shoots, and interviewing a bevy of designers for monthly feature articles. Suddenly, my job was my passion. I loved it!

Managing the fashion department also provided the experience I needed to learn how to forecast style trends, and develop and maintain relationships with designers, showrooms, and retailers. Those relationships, in turn, provided me with the opportunity to style normal girls (not just model types) who needed help finding clothes, putting looks together, and just generally figuring out what to do with their wardrobe. Nothing made me happier than seeing a client's happy face as we reinvented a less-than-perfect closet, or found just the right look for a big-time event.

As a journalist and stylist, and having now spent many years watching fashion trends come and go, I feel as though, in helping others achieve a style that is just right for them, I've found the perfect blend of my experience and my abilities. And throughout these years in the industry, I've discovered the secret to style (shhh!): No matter where you shop, how much money you have, or what you look like in a designer gown, you need to figure out, firstly, who you are, and secondly, what it is that makes you feel totally confident and comfortable in your own skin.

And that's why I wrote *The Book of Styling*. I want to show you how to succeed in styling yourself, and—if you really love it—how to style others and even launch your career. This book is meant to build your styling confidence, inspire you, change your attitude about fashion, and just generally teach you all you need to know to set you on your own (more fashionable) way. The tips and tricks I've gathered throughout my own style journey will be shared, including how to look like a million bucks when you're broke (a topic I honed while spending my 20s living in one of the most expensive cities in the world), and the best way to inventory and add to your collection (also known as that pile of clothes on the floor of your closet). Along the way you'll learn a ton, and hopefully also gain a new perspective on what it means to dress well. And, above all, I encourage you to have fun—because in the end life is about much more than just a closet full of clothes!

Somer Flaherty

Table of Contents

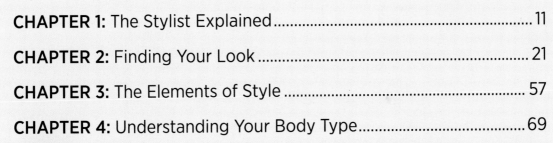

Part I: Style Gets Personal

Part II: Style Goes to Work

Part I:
Style Gets Personal

There's no such thing as "perfect style." Style is about the journey, not the destination. So whether you're naturally stylish or naturally style-less, there's always room for improvement. The key to enhancing your own style is figuring out what works for you—but that's easier said than done.

Part I is here to help you determine your own personal sense of style. In this first section you'll learn about the history of styling and the key elements of styling, and you'll also learn how to achieve a variety of iconic looks, and how to make those looks work for your own particular body type. Then, once you know who your inspirations are, what kind of look compliments your body type, and what your scene is all about, you can take it to the streets (with the help of Part II). So good luck, and happy styling!

CHAPTER 1

The Stylist Explained

The clothes, shoes, purses, and jewelry that you wear—and the way you combine those elements together—is, collectively, what's known as "style." But style is more than just an outfit: Your own individual style is a way to express your personality and tell the world just who you are. And the process of creating an outfit (aka your "look") isn't just a necessary duty before you start your day, it's also a very revealing action. How you choose what you'll wear—a color that makes you feel good, a piece of jewelry that evokes a great memory, or a dress that reminds you of a favorite celebrity—can say a lot about what you value, your goals, and what makes you, you.

Style might not have the respect of other artistic endeavors like painting, writing, or dancing, but for a lot of people, it provides an even more important function: It's what sets you apart from the pack, and if you think about getting dressed as a daily performance rather than a chore, you may start to realize that clothes (and accessories) can convey both who you are and who you want to be. That's why we have phrases like "Dress for success," and "Dress for the job you want, not the one you have." It's also the reason why it's so hard to dress for a first date, and why brides often spend more money on a wedding dress—an item that will only be worn once—than on any other piece of clothing they will ever own. The fact is, we know how important clothing is, even when we're not actively thinking about it.

STYLING: A BRIEF OVERVIEW

Because self-presentation is so important, many people choose to enlist the help of a professional stylist. Think of a stylist as a kind of puzzle master. Stylists have to consider budget, availability, and location, and also take all the variables that make a person unique—like body type, hair color, and complexion—and figure out a way to create the best possible look for their clients. When you feel good about what you're wearing, you also feel in control of who you are. And although stylists are often hired to help other people craft the perfect style, you can hone the same set of skills and tactics that the professionals use to style yourself.

The Birth of the Stylist

DNA studies have revealed that our ancestors started regularly wearing clothes about 170,000 years ago. But style is about more than clothes, and if you wanted to put a year on the birth of modern styling, you'd have to fast forward to the Industrial Revolution, when clothing became much easier to make and everyday people began to take fashion into their own hands.

The arrival of fashion magazines like *Vogue* and *Harper's Bazaar* helped to support the growing fashion industry, but the key moment didn't arrive until 1933, when *Harper's Bazaar* editor-in-chief, Carmel Snow, debuted the first on-location photo shoot. His photographer, Martin Munkacsi, took pictures of a model at a beach, whereas previously, almost all fashion shoots were done in a studio with carefully staged models and preselected clothes. This first on-location shoot made fashion magazine history, and it also made the role of stylist even more important to the fashion world.

But it wasn't until the explosion of gossipy tabloid magazines in the mid 1990s that the profession of styling became really well-known. Celebrities, afraid of being criticized in tabloids' "worst-dressed" lists, hired professional dressers to create dramatic red carpet looks. And as media coverage ramped up and began to intrude on celebrities' personal lives, they started using stylists for help with everyday wear, as well.

The State of Styling Today

Luckily for us, you don't have to be a celebrity to have great style. Think of it this way: There are many things you don't have any control over—like bad weather, delayed flights, traffic, and pop quizzes. So when you do find an area of your life where you can be completely in charge, it's empowering to seize the opportunity and take the reins. Fashion provides exactly this type of opportunity, and the best part is that it's available for everyone to grab hold of. As opposed to the 19th century, when waists had to be squeezed into tiny corsets, or in the '80s and '90s, when designer fashions were only available to the wealthiest clients, great style is now accessible to anyone who wants to look for it.

There are budget-friendly shops that carry gently loved items from big-name brands, department stores that have a rotating list of limited-time-only designer collections at a fraction of the normal retail price, and even the not-to-be-missed neighborhood garage sale, where one woman's stash of seasoned cardigans is your *au courant* vintage find.

Size, once a past hurdle to the opportunity for great style, is also much less of a barrier now. Not only are models like Crystal Renn (who at a healthy 165 pounds graced the covers of *Vogue* and *Harper's Bazaar*) gaining in popularity, but major fashion lines like Marc Jacobs are also beginning to create lines for women that don't stop at size 16.

For women of any size, location was also once a roadblock to style. At the end of the 19th century, unless your parents received the Sears Roebuck & Co. Catalogue—which sold everything from cough syrup to barn paint to clothing—your fashion choices were limited to the fabric you had and what you could sew. Now, thanks to the internet and overnight shipping, you can shop virtually anywhere and anytime, and be wearing your new clothes the very next day. Just more proof that change isn't always a bad thing.

What This All Means For You

With access to fashion comes access to a world of your own making, where it doesn't necessarily matter where you come from, what type of body you have, where you live, or even how old you are. You can choose your own adventure!

So what are you waiting for?! Styling opportunities are everywhere! Have you ever helped a friend choose the perfect prom dress or added a twist to your school uniform with head-to-toe accessories? You may not know it, but you're already acting like a stylist. A stylist isn't just someone who's paid to dress celebrities or the super rich, but a persona you can take on each day when you dress yourself. And if you work hard enough, you even may be able to turn your passion for the perfect outfit into a career!

Later in this book we'll discuss styling internships and opportunities in all facets of fashion (including jobs at magazines, photographic work, and personal styling ideas). But before any of that's possible, you'll need to master some key styling tools and learn the basic characteristics that make a stylist successful.

STYLING TRAITS

No matter what area of the fashion industry a stylist works in, there are still a few key traits that every stylist has to have. A good way to remember them is with the acronym TREND, which breaks up into five key attributes:

T: Truthful

R: Reasonable

E: Exciting

N: Never neglectful of the necessities

D: Detail oriented

Truthful: Whether you want to give advice to others or just style yourself, you need to be honest about what works and what doesn't. Just because an item is a trend or has a designer label doesn't mean it's the best option for a specific look or person.

Reasonable: We all wish we had never-ending credit card limits with no repercussions to over spending, but that doesn't look like it's going to happen anytime soon. Until then, you have to be reasonable about what your budget is and what you (or you client) can afford. Anyone can look good with a head-to-toe, off-the-runway look, but a great stylist has to be able to succeed on a treasure hunt at more wallet-friendly locations, as well.

Exciting: If we all looked the same, the world would be a pretty boring place. Don't be afraid to experiment with fashion or be the first person in your neighborhood or school to interpret a new trend, or reinterpret a classic look.

Never neglectful of the necessities: Trend items are fun, but necessary pieces like a little black dress or a perfect pair of jeans will last. The key to great style is having a mix of both trendy and necessary pieces in the closet.

Detail oriented: A stylist has to be in command of all the elements that make up a single look, including the budget, the personality, the occasion, and the body type.

Being Confident With Your Own Style

Even once you've mastered the traits of a great stylist, you have to be confident in your own style before you can style others. You may not have been born in a Diane von Furstenberg wrap dress, rocking Jimmy Choo stilettos, and carrying a Hermes Birkin bag, but neither were most fashion insiders; they developed their style through years of practice.

Fashion can be interpreted in many different ways. You may think the kitten heel is outdated, while your best friend might believe it's the perfect choice to give a little lift (literally) to pedestrian flats. No matter how "out of fashion" a piece of clothing is, if every time you put it on you feel amazing, then you shouldn't ever give it up. In fact, an item like that deserves prime real estate: a spot in the front of your closet.

And no matter what style you end up rocking, remember that whether you're a size 4 or 14 styling can both complement your body and actually solve some teen-life bummers. Not the most popular girl in class? Didn't get the lead role in the school play? It doesn't matter. With fashion you can be anyone you want to be, right now. You don't have to wait to get older, graduate from college, or land your dream job. It's a fantasyland where you can be a Goth Girl one day, and a Surfer Chick or a Glamour Gal the next. Sure, learning how to style a great look isn't going to help you pass your midterms or save the world, but great style can give you the confidence to meet new people, sign up for an after-school club, ace your internship interview, or even just smile a little larger. And the best part about style is that it's always changing. The clothing you choose today doesn't have to define your look forever.

Riding High in Heels

Although high heels are a seemingly female-driven trend, men were actually the first to wear the shoes. High heels appeared in France in the late 1500s and were used to help keep a man's feet in the stirrups when riding a horse. As an added benefit, when walking, the extra height managed to raise him a couple of inches above the waste-filled streets of the time.

THIS BOOK CAN HELP YOU GET STARTED

This book is meant to be your own practical guide to styling. You'll learn how to wrangle a wardrobe, manage a budget, curate your closet, and avoid fashion mistakes and budget pitfalls. And you'll find out what cuts, styles, and silhouettes fit your body best, along with tips, tricks, and tools of the trade.

As you begin working your way through the book, you may notice a fashion evolution starting to take place. You'll begin to experiment with colors (blacks and browns can be worn together!) and trends you never would have dared before, and you might actually like the results!

As you begin your life as a stylist, try debuting new looks in low-key places like a friend's slumber party or a movie night, and stick with your tried-and-true outfits for things like yearbook photos. And remember, have fun!

Fashion Action
Create a Mood Board

A mood board—also known as an inspiration board, or style board—is really just a blank slate (or in this case, probably a blank bulletin board) on which to figure out, in a very abstract kind of way, what you want a given look to feel like. Designers and stylists use mood boards to help find inspiration for an upcoming collection or even for a single look at a big event.

WHAT YOU'LL NEED

- Magazines
- Pieces of fabric
- Photos
- Runway images
- Colored markers/pens
- Scissors
- Tape, glue, or pushpins
- Somewhere to post everything that inspires you: corkboard, poster board, a wall, or large sheet of paper

WHAT TO INCLUDE

Anything that inspires you! Some ideas to get you started would include:

- a favorite saying or phrase
- tear-outs from magazines
- runway images
- ideas from fashion blogs
- fabric or color swatches

The board should be more metaphorical than literal. Just because you have a picture of a horse on your mood board doesn't mean your outfit should feature saddles, or that your look will necessarily lean toward cowboy-wear. Instead, the horse could represent freedom, strength, or even just the cream, brown, and sepia-toned colors you want to include in the look.

HOW TO DO IT

Your mood board should spark your creativity and provide new inspirational angles. It doesn't have to be perfect, but should fit your personality as well as your style. Don't be too concerned with how neat and organized the final product is.

HOW TO USE IT

Have fun with your mood board and be open to adding anything in fashion that catches your eye. The finished result can be used to hone in on a chosen color palette or aid in picking out textures and even the era of your outfit.

TIP

If you want to add something to your mood board on the go or carry it with you everywhere, apps exist for creating a mood board on your tablet or smartphone. Also, online sites like Polyvore.com allow users to create their own virtual mood boards.

CHAPTER 2

Finding Your Look

Your fashion personality is the key to discovering what kind of time you want to invest in your style. For example, some girls just don't feel comfortable if their nail polish doesn't match their outfit, while others wouldn't waste a second even thinking about it. Neither approach is wrong; each is just a reflection of a different fashion personality.

Perhaps the reason you're not analyzing polish colors is because you're too busy with a part-time job or a club soccer team. But figuring out your fashion personality is important because it can help you choose looks that complement your lifestyle—the two really go hand-in-hand. And if you're unsure of what your fashion personality is, then just take the quiz below to find out what type of approach will work best with your life!

QUIZ: WHAT'S YOUR FASHION PERSONALITY?

1. On a typical school day you:

   A. Wake up with just a few minutes to spare and grab the first stain-free outfit on the floor.

   B. Get out of bed with enough time to try on a few different outfits and see which one looks best.

   C. Set aside a block of your morning to check the weather report, base your clothing options around it, and repaint your nails to match your shoes.

2. When choosing a prom dress you:

   A. Let your mom or big sister pick something out, since they have great taste anyway.

   B. Go shopping with a group of friends and spend a fun day finding a great dress.

   C. Study red carpet looks, sketch out your own design, and hire a tailor to create a one-of-a-kind dress.

3. On average you wear a pair of jeans:

   A. Almost every day since they're comfy and durable.

   B. Two to three times per week, with a variety of tops.

   C. Almost never. If it's not on the runway it's not on you.

4. When working out you usually wear:

   A. Something baggy and breathable.

   B. One of four to five key pieces that show off the work-out's results.

   C. Something from a full dresser filled with color-coordinated spandex, Lycra, and loose-fitting cotton choices.

5. Your biggest fashion concern is:

   A. There just isn't enough time to dress how you want.

   B. You like how you dress but would love to give your style a bit more excitement.

   C. You aren't sure if your closet should be color coordinated or organized alphabetically by designer.

KEY:

Mostly A's: Just Not That Into It

To you, the question "what should I wear?!" is about as exciting as a trip to the dentist. But dressing doesn't have to be a routine time drain. Try having a few uniforms in your closet. Not the awful plaid skirt and sweater type of uniform; just three or four outfits that you absolutely love. Make sure the looks are in solid colors and casual enough to wear every day. (For example, a great pair of jeans and a well-cut black top could be one of your uniforms.)

These are the looks that will make you feel great every time you wear them, and chances are that you love these pieces because the cut and style really fit your body type. Work these uniforms into your wardrobe from now on. There's no shame in having a handful of go-to outfits that you can pull from your closet with ease—especially when you've hit the alarm's snooze button a few too many times already.

Mostly B's: Style-ish

Sure, you try and pick the right outfit for the occasion, but you aren't stressing over the details. That's great, but fashion should also be exciting. Your goal should be to focus on your everyday personal style. Concentrate on a few exciting (think colorful, eye-catching, or unique) pieces that look good on you and really stand out. We'll call these items your spotlight pieces. Try and integrate at least one spotlight piece into your wardrobe every day.

This doesn't just mean incorporating the trendiest item in your closet. It means adding that amazing hand-beaded bracelet you picked up at a flea market to your everyday skinny-jeans-and-vintage-cardigan look. There's no mistaking a girl who likes what she's wearing. Be proud of your look and you'll sparkle.

Mostly C's: Fashion Fiend

You have a sixth sense for putting together a look. It's an instinct for you, and hunting down the perfect accessory is as necessary as breathing. But here's a big fashion secret: Perfection just isn't possible. And even if you managed everything to the last detail, it's probably the most unfashionable thing you could do. Eventually, that kind of attention will take the fun out of fashion. So leave room for a bit of unexpected creativity. Try to avoid relentlessly pursuing the newest and trendiest pieces, and think twice before you buy something you think you have to have. Instead, work on creating a signature collection—key pieces that you'll incorporate and build upon in your day's look. Not only will choosing what you're going to wear be quicker (and a lot more fun), but you'll also start to gravitate toward looks that truly suit you (instead of what happens to flatter your favorite celebs).

No matter what type of fashion personality you have (or are working toward), remember that it's all about you. With fashion you can dress like anyone you want to be. But knowing how you want to represent yourself and how much time and energy you want to devote to your look are important first steps.

FINDING INSPIRATION

Now that you know what your fashion personality is and what works for your lifestyle, the next step is to find inspiration and new ideas. Don't worry, you don't have to look far. You can find inspiration almost anywhere, from the lacrosse field to the drama club to a night out at the movies. Here are some additional "real world" places you should be able to draw some inspiration from.

1. Coffee Shops

People-watching is one of the best ways to see how a variety of outfits are put together, and it's hard to find a better place to people-watch than the local coffee shop. Coffee shops are especially helpful because they're so casual; most patrons are just wearing their typical everyday outfits, which can provide a lot of inspiration for your daily wear.

Don't miss: The barista's style sense. These employees often set the tone for the shop's overall look and feel.

2. Football Games

Surprised? But it's true: Any setting where people show school or team spirit is a great place to see unique interpretations of everyday style—especially when it comes to the use of color. Many fashionistas get bogged down in head-to-toe black. If you look beyond the standard jerseys, sports fans often find creative ways to wear bright color combinations.

Don't miss: The on-the-field style of sports reporters. These folks know how to dress stylishly for any type of weather.

3. Art Galleries

It's hard to find a single building with as much creativity as an art gallery. Strolling the space, you may find it's actually the other patrons that provide you with a new perspective on angles, colors, and textures.

Don't miss: Special gallery events like receptions for new exhibits or evenings with the artist for an insider's look at the inspiration behind the art.

4. The Library

Many designers and stylists will study magazines to gain inspiration for new styles. But purchasing magazines each month can get expensive, and lots of older editions aren't available online. Luckily for us, most public libraries have a hefty collection of current and past titles that you can sift through for new styling ideas.

Don't miss: The historical books section, where you can view drawings of past style icons like Marie Antoinette and Cleopatra.

5. New Neighborhoods

When you live in the same neighborhood for a long time, you get used to the style you see everyday. Get out of your bubble and walk around a section of town that's completely new to you, or that feels totally different. If you live uptown, spend the day drinking coffee and window-shopping downtown. And if your neighborhood has a laid back, bohemian vibe, try strolling your city's financial district for a peek into the life of a buttoned-up suit.

Don't miss: Having a meal in the new neighborhood; it's an easy and natural way to study local fashion.

NEED MORE INSPIRATION?

If you're still in need of inspiration, try turning to technology. Without ever leaving home you can check out popular fashion sites and blogs, or even use your smart phone to check out new trends from all over the world.

1. The Sartorialist (TheSartorialist.com)

Scott Schuman chronicles stylish everyday people for his blog. He wanders the streets of Manhattan, Milan, and just about anywhere else to photograph cool people wearing cool clothes. These aren't pics of socialites swathed in designer labels, but men and women with confidence and a distinctive personal style. Scott's blog also landed him a gig at *GQ*, where you can see how his everyday insights impact fashion's elite as well.

Don't miss: Comments from Sartorialist devotees—it's not unusual for Scott's daily images to get pages of posted feedback. Studying the feedback is a great way to figure out what really stands out in an outfit.

2. Style (Style.com)

As one of the best sites for runway coverage, style.com also features trend reporting, fashion news, and interactive fashion discussion forums. For an even more immediate experience, head to the site's video section for highlights from catwalks around the world, along with interviews with designers and models.

Don't miss: The archives of runway images organized by designer. It's a great place to get a sense of how a designer's aesthetic has developed over the years.

3. Garance Doré (GaranceDore.fr/en)

Named one of *French Vogue* website's "40 Women of the Decade," along-side Lady Gaga and Angelina Jolie, the street-style blogger (who is dating and living with Scott Schuman of the Sartorialist) uses a mix of portrait photography, illustrations, and reporting to give you an inside look at the musings of a female fashion insider.

Don't miss: Practicing your bilingual skills with the French language version of the blog at GaranceDore.fr. Paris is the fashion capital of the world, after all (although some in LA, Milan, and New York might disagree).

4. Polyvore (Polyvore.com)

Think of this site as your own personal style collage. Want to know if a strappy pair of gladiator flats, silk cargo shorts, and an off-the-shoulder cashmere blouse combine nicely? Place the product images together on your own blank slate to create what Polyvore calls a set.

Don't miss: If you want to rock your virtual look in the real world, just click on the relevant item from your collage and Polyvore will take you to the site that sells it.

5. Pose (phone app)

This smart-phone app allows you to view looks from other users who post images of their favorite clothing, shoes, or accessories. Follow users with a style that you admire, or check out Pose's featured users section for daily style inspiration.

Don't miss: Posting your own looks and getting feedback from users around the world (who then have the ability to "love" your pose). If a particular look gets a ton of love, you know you've got a winner.

THE LOWDOWN ON DIFFERENT LOOKS

True inspiration gives you the chance to think outside of yourself and create looks that you never would have come up with otherwise. You may find yourself identifying with one type of fashion character or overlapping into a few different characters. The following list isn't definitive, but it does include some of the most popular fashion types, each with extensive wardrobe options. Where do you see yourself in these categories?

The Glam Girl
*(for when the only difference between a
Tuesday and a prom is a corsage)*

Classic, classy looks—the kind worn by silver screen stars Marlene Dietrich and Marilyn Monroe in the '40s and '50s—are at the forefront of the Glam Girl's closet. The ultimate Glamour Girl uniform is a spotlight-worthy dress, but one of the biggest misconceptions about this fashion character is that it begins and ends with a dress. In fact, there are plenty of chic alternatives—like silk separates, retro polka-dot blouses, tailored high-waist trousers, chic wraps, detailed cardigans, and pencil skirts. Whichever wardrobe pieces you choose, keep the look glamour-approved by paying special attention to the fit and appearance of the garments. If steaming or ironing a wrinkled frock is needed, take the time and do it— you can't get away with seemingly disheveled garments the way the Grunge Gal can.

How to Make It Work: Diamonds may be a Glamour Girl's best friend, but rhinestones can do the same work for less. Play up the look with a sparkling rhinestone brooch, an oversized cocktail ring (faux of course), and dangling, chandelier-style earrings. If it's an evening event, long satin gloves or a thick Japanese-style obi belt are nice additions. But during the day, you can still soak up the sparkle in delicately sequined cardigans, embroidered Pashmina wraps, tanks with a subtle sheen, and wedges in place of sky-high heels.

Tips for the Glamour Girl: With a few modifications, glamour can work in almost any setting. When you're at the beach, let your high-waisted swimsuit peek out through the silhouette of a sheer beaded cover-up. At brunch with friends, stick with a flattering wrap dress in cotton, and pair it with attractive flats. Try and build a formidable glamour pant collection with high-waisted, wide-legged pants. The resulting silhouette is always appropriate, and as an added bonus, the style helps to elongate the look of your legs.

To pull off the high-waisted look, keep the waist-band of the pant sitting at your belly button, and choose a style with a center crease and a wide-leg flare that flows from the hip.

Body Type Alert: The Glam Girl look knows no boundaries when it comes to body types. (For more on body types, see Chapter 4.) However, because dresses are a key part of this fashion character's wardrobe, pay attention to the styles of dresses that flatter your body. If you want to accentuate your upper body, try a strapless or halter-style dress. Then, for areas that you don't want to accentuate, choose styles that offer figure-friendly draping.

As with any look, one of the most important factors is the fit. Don't even think about leaving the house in something that feels suffocating. If you can't bear the thought of giving up a piece despite a bad fit, see if a reasonably priced tailor can either let out some of the material (to give you some breathing room) or make some reductions (if it's too big).

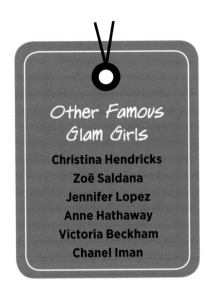

Other Famous Glam Girls

Christina Hendricks
Zoë Saldana
Jennifer Lopez
Anne Hathaway
Victoria Beckham
Chanel Iman

Case in Point: Blake Lively
She's been featured on multiple covers of *Vogue* magazine, is friend to many of the biggest names in the fashion design world, and has been a Versace-clad attendee at the annual Metropolitan Museum of Art Costume Institute Ball (one of the top glam fashion events of the year). But when *Vogue* Editor Anna Wintour introduced Blake Lively to designer Karl Lagerfeld during a couture fashion week, that's when things got serious. The high school cheerleader turned *Gossip Girl* actress was soon part of the inner circle, as an ambassador for Lagerfeld's Chanel brand. Besides getting invited to all the best parties, the ambassador role included a stint as the face of *Mademoiselle*'s handbag advertising campaign—and it doesn't get much more glamorous than that.

The Socialite

(for the girl who thinks resort wear is a year-round necessity)

Think of the Socialite as the Glam Girl's distant cousin. Both have a propensity to dress up more than other fashion characters, but the real difference here is that the Socialite's fashion style includes a range of polished yet casual items, like a jersey belted Grecian dress, tailored wide-legged pants, deck shoes, and a utilitarian shirt dress that would feel right at home on yachts, private jets, and fancy luncheons. Don't let your bank account balance—or lack thereof—dissuade you from attempting the Socialite look; it's really more about confidence than wealth. Socialites are constantly schmoozing at parties, being photographed in the local press, and hosting a never-ending list of charity events, so they have to be "on" all the time. The key to this look: Stand-up tall, own it, and of course, smile.

How to Make It Work: There have been many great couples throughout history: Romeo and Juliet, Sonny and Cher, and Bella Swan and Edward Cullen—but the Socialite and the handbag should also be included in that list. Whether it's a satchel, tote, or clutch, the handbag is the number one accessory to complete this look. Avoid bags that appear to be walking advertisements, with logos emblazoned on every square inch, and instead stick to more understated examples.

When choosing other accessories, make sure that the item is noteworthy but still appropriate to a minimalist aesthetic—so no buckles with showy designer names, please. With a skirt or dress, try pairing opaque tights (in colors like gray, black, or mocha) with ankle-high booties. And every stylish socialite knows that she can't leave the house without her sunglasses. But again, whichever style you choose, pick a pair that doesn't have colossal logos on the side.

Tips for the Socialite: You don't have to attend Paris' annual Crillon Ball (the annual gathering of a select group of international young society gals) to dress like a socialite. Although a couture budget isn't something most would turn down, great style doesn't have to be expensive. The Socialite's look can be achieved on any budget. Thrift stores can be a great place for tailored pants, blazers, and blouses. Designer pieces can be scored for a fraction of the cost at consignment stores, and one-size-fits-all accessories like handbags, belts, and costume jewelry can probably be borrowed from someone in your family.

Body Type Alert: The Socialite look is polished and poised, which makes the fit of the outfit very important. To really pull off this look you can't get away with anything that's even a bit too big or too small. (For more information on dressing for your body shape, check out Chapter 4.) Stick with pants that don't crease or gather at the front of the thighs (a sign you need to move up a size) and avoid any dress that requires more than one person to aid in zipping up (just one of many signs that the item doesn't fit).

Other Famous Socialites

Tatiana Santo Domingo
Nicky Hilton
Olivia Palermo
Lily Collins

Case in Point: Kate Middleton
Kate Middleton, known formally as Catherine, Duchess of Cambridge, belongs at the top of any socialite's fashion hierarchy. Her casual elegance is always on display—whether she's spending a day at the polo field, watching a tennis match at Wimbledon, or meeting with presidents, prime ministers, and other palace types. Perhaps the ultimate show of style came on Kate's wedding day. With an estimated 8,500 journalists in London to cover her wedding to Prince William (and millions of people watching from their televisions at home), Kate walked down the aisle in an Alexander McQueen frock—with an almost nine-foot train—complete with lace and ivory silk tulle. For the post-wedding party Kate slipped into another McQueen dress, this time a party-ready strapless white satin evening gown with diamond-like detailing around the waist and a cozy white shrug to keep her warm in the chilly London weather.

The Tomboy

for girls who like to wear a tie every once in a while)

The Tomboy's style can sometimes look androgynous—like when you throw on a simple T-shirt and jeans—but at other times it captures the full menswear experience, with a bow tie, suit jacket, and even cuff links. The style isn't anything new. Marlene Dietrich was known to rock a tuxedo in the 1920s, and in 1966 designer Yves Saint Laurent created the famous "Le Smoking" tuxedo jacket for women.

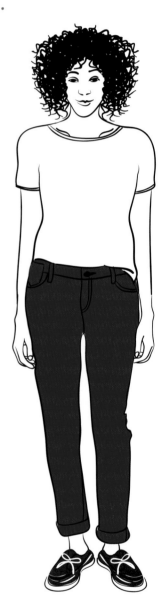

How to Make It Work: You have a wide variety of material choices with the Tomboy look, but when it comes to colors, try and stick to hues like blue, black, gray, neutrals, and red instead of the more traditionally feminine pinks and pastels. One of the best places to try this look is at a formal occasion where you can ditch the dress and opt for cool trousers accessorized with a bow tie and an oversized watch. If you have to bring a purse, downsize and stick with a clutch or miniature pouch. If you have too much gear, stick with a style like the flap clutch, which appears small in size but holds more items than you would think—it has material that is folded in half but opens to reveal double the room. For pants, try slim-cut tuxedo trousers with a tonal trim (like a black satin strip on black wool pants) that sit at your natural waist. For a dressy occasion, a button-down blouse (short sleeve or long sleeve) with structured collar and cuffs can pair nicely with the tuxedo trousers.

Tips for the Tomboy: The closets of your brother, dad, or uncle all offer the perfect breeding ground for the Tomboy. Try one-size-fits-all pieces like a tie or fedora hat first, and then try belting an oversized collared men's shirt and pair with leggings for a new take on the tunic. When you are shopping for tomboy-worthy additions to your wardrobe, choose styles that are menswear influenced but still fit the female shape—something that can be achieved by tailoring and slim fits. Jeans, which you probably aren't able to get away with borrowing from your brother or dad, should sit at your natural waist (no low-low hip-hugger styles here) and offer enough room for your thighs to breathe. When choosing a jean, look for styles with distressed detailing like fading (to give it a well-loved feel) and simple stitching on the back pockets (forget about any rhinestones). Heels aren't a no-no with the tomboy look, but more natural styles include an ankle boot (in faux or real leather) or a classic slip-on driving shoe (looks kind of like a moccasin) with stand-out stitching and a rubber sole.

Body Type Alert: The ubiquitous jeans and T-shirt look is a perfect fit for any body type, but be careful to retain your shape with the outfit. No one looks good swimming in a sea of fabric. And because pants are key with this look, tall and petite gals should pay special attention to where the pant leg falls. (See Chapter 4 to learn more about dressing for your body type.) Most dry cleaners offer simple tailoring services to shorten the pant leg or even let the hemline out to provide extra inches in length.

Other Famous Tomboys

Diane Keaton
Ellen Page
Kristen Stewart
Samantha Ronson
Patti Smith
Ellen Degeneres

Case in Point: Agyness Deyn
It isn't just her bleached short hair (which she has been known to completely shave off) that makes Agyness an icon. Famous for projecting a stylish boyish vibe even when she's not walking the catwalk, the supermodel—called the "British tomboy-in-chief" by *Vogue*—has been spotted reporting for modeling jobs in tailored three-piece suits, and donning a single-breasted black trouser suit at a big Hollywood film premiere. Her modeling career has also capitalized on her look. She has been the face of tomboy favorite Dr. Martens advertising campaigns, and the magazine *i-D* devoted an entire issue to her—the first time in its almost 30-year history it had ever done such a thing.

The 1930s

Style Through the Decades

The Great Depression, which followed the stock market crash of 1929, brought about huge changes in fashion. And the tomboy look was perhaps the ultimate symbol of these shifting styles. Katharine Hepburn, Marlene Dietrich, and aviation pioneer Amelia Earhart all pioneered the style. But it was Earhart, who was often photographed in her signature tomboy look—a leather jacket, fitted pants, and a silk tie around her neck—who is the most iconic. Earhart also had her own fashion collection, which featured budget-conscious clothes with practical, easy-to-wear fabrics.

The Preppy Girl
(for all the hostessess with the mostesses)

You don't have to be named Chip, Muffy, or Buffy to appreciate Preppy style. This classic all-American look can be worn by anyone, as long as you are comfortable in the kind of conservative, demure styles (think polo T-shirts, pearls, polka dots, trousers, and blazers) that feel right at home at croquet matches, sailing races, the stables, and a weekend in the Hamptons.

How to Make It Work: Pop your shirt collar and think "casual resort-wear meets Easter formal" to pull this look off. Key colors include bubblegum pink, mint green, canary yellow, and tropical turquoise. During the winter months (or on a day at sea) add water-resistant deck shoes, with a rounded toe, rubber sole, and all the trimmings. And remember, for true preppy style, skin is not in. You will need to embrace modesty (gasp!) with below-the-knee skirts and dresses, higher-waisted pants, and even blazers. Remember, grandma approves of almost everything the Preppy wants to wear.

Tips for the Preppy Girl: Fun floral shifts in turquoise and tangerine and fuchsia—colors and style made popular by socialite Lilly Pulitzer, who, after opening a fresh-squeezed juice stand in the 1960s, decided she needed bright hues in her wardrobe to hide the fruit splashes. The cheerful dresses were so popular with her customers that she started selling them. Think outside of your traditional locale and purchase items through catalogs, which are great places to shop for preppy classics like oversized book totes monogrammed with your initials. Hitting up your local craft store for supplies can also be a good way to get in touch with your inner prep-approved Martha Stewart; stock up on supplies and materials to create your own grosgrain ribbon belts and fabric headbands.

Body Type Alert: As with any look, fit is an integral part of preppy style. For gals with a full bust, try full skirts with subtle details like beading or ribbon at the hemline to help balance out the bottom half (more on balancing body shapes in Chapter 4). For those with a straighter, rectangular frame (where there's little change in width between the bust, waist, and hip), try fitted combos like skinny pants and a tailored polo paired with deck shoes. And polo styles aren't just for shirts—the polo dress complete with collar and button-front detailing also works well. Just choose a style that isn't too clingy to the hips and stomach area. For dressier occasions when a blazer is required (day at the country club?), search local thrift stores for a schoolboy uniform style in navy or plaid. These classic (usually cotton-blend) blazers offer a lighter weight style than a traditional business suit blazer, which should provide a bit more comfort. Check the fit of the armholes (not too tight or too loose) and the length of the sleeves (either at the wrist or right below or right above the elbow).

Other Famous Preppies

Elle Fanning
Hailee Steinfeld
Emma Watson
Kate Beckinsale
Julia Stiles

Case in Point: Natalie Portman
You may know her as Queen Amidala in the *Star Wars* prequels, or as Nina, the schizo ballerina in *Black Swan*, but Academy Award–winning actress Natalie Portman also has some serious preppy credentials. After earning straight A's in high school, she went on to study neuroscience at Harvard University (an enduring preppy hot zone). Unlike other young Hollywood starlets who tend to show a lot of skin, Natalie's everyday style leans heavily on fitted jeans and windbreakers—but that doesn't mean she's afraid of the occasional red carpet outfit from Rodarte or Lanvin (two prep-approved designers). And just because her dress is more conservative than other starlets doesn't mean the actress has lackluster style—who else could get Dior to produce specially made vegan heels just for her, so she could still wear the brand without sacrificing her ideals.

The Hipster
(if you think you aren't one, then you probably are)

How much more stylish can you get? Th**e** *American Heritage Dictionary* defines the word "hipster" as: "One who is exceptionally aware of or interested in the latest trends and tastes." And although the *New York Times* editor Philip B. Corbett asked for the term to be given "some rest," it doesn't really seem like that's going to happen anytime soon. There's nothing that quite encompasses the style. It's essentially eclectic but distinct enough that everyone knows what it is.

How to Make It Work: You don't have to be a vegan, bike messenger, or design blogger to pull off the hipster vibe, but you do have to have enough style to share a common field of cool with these people. The most ubiquitous elements of hipster style include simple pieces like skinny jeans, wayfarer sunglasses, button-front menswear shirts, and leather jackets. The real excitement is in the accessories: vintage purses, messenger bags, and clip-in hair tinsel or feather hair extensions. To truly pull off the vibe, you also have to exude the Hipster personality. When you're rocking a pair of '80s sunglasses, a leather jacket from your mom's teenage groupie days, and just about any blouse from your grandmother's closet (oh, so hipster), you've got to believe that your look is as stylish as haute couture.

Tips for the Hipster: Luckily for your budget, designer clothing is the antithesis of hipster style. Scour the racks at your local thrift stores and piles of clothing at neighborhood garage sales for gently used pieces. Subtle graphic print tees of a past concert, or a defunct sports team logo, or long-off-the-air television show can suddenly become cool again! If you already wear eyeglasses, you may be able to find a discarded oversized dark-rimmed pair you can take to your optometrist to replace with your own prescription lenses. If you don't technically need glasses, you are still in luck. An optometrist can replace the prescription lenses with clear (nonprescription) lenses or dark lenses for custom sunglasses. For your handbag, score a vintage bowling ball bag or doctor's bag, an oversized hobo, or a tattered bike messenger style. Just be sure to leave the fancy clutches at home. And for jewelry, add a rubber wristband printed with your favorite cause or underground musician's name.

Body Type Alert: You've got to be comfortable flaunting your legs to pull off a pair of skinny jeans (more about that in Chapter 4), but for gals not looking to enhance their gams, there are still plenty of solid hipster options available, like a loose-fitting romper, for instance. The perfect fit of a T-shirt shouldn't be underestimated. In fact, it was so important to hipster Ashley Olsen and her sister Mary-Kate that they created their own fashion label, Elizabeth and James (named after the twins' siblings), to produce one. Pick a shirt that falls just below the waistline of your pants, with just enough room to not cling to your stomach or fit more than a hand's length from your stomach to the outstretched fabric of the shirt. When done right, worn alone or layered under chunky knits, the T-shirt is a hipster staple.

Other Famous Hipsters

Michelle Williams
M.I.A.
Rachel Bilson
Chloë Sevigny
Zooey Deschanel

Case in Point: Alexa Chung
The ultimate British hipster, Alexa Chung is a model, actress, some-time fashion designer, and writer. She's known as a muse for Chanel's Karl Lagerfeld and says the Hollywood glamour thing makes her sick. Adding to her hipster cred, Alexa is also said to be filming a television series about scouring thrift stores, yard sales, and flea markets for vintage clothing. And when a red-carpet worthy dress didn't show up in time for the CFDA/Vogue Fashion Fund Awards (a big-time celeb gala), Alexa (who doesn't use a professional stylist anyway), did what any self-respecting hipster would do: She captivated the audience in a simple pair of black shorts with a white button-down shirt. The fashion world has taken notice of Alexa's style—she's been named a best-dressed woman of the year by *Vogue*, and a number of blogs now chronicle her every stylish move.

The Sporty Girl
(for the next Lisa Leslie)

Far from the '80s style spandex one-pieces and sweat headbands, the modern take on the sporty look can include everything from a fashionable tennis skirt (a la Stella McCartney) and simple tank, to knee-high athletic socks with running short-shorts. The key is to achieve a balance between real on-field wear and fashionable updates.

How to Make It Work: Don't overlook the importance of shoes for sporty style. Put away the stilettos and platforms and embrace the new sneaker—one that involves elements like art, color, and, yes, good old fashioned function. For your purse, forget about the satchel or clutch and switch to a smaller-sized version of the traditional gym bag, which will translate well from dinner with the gals to dance class. Look for details like vented compartments (your sneakers and heels won't stink), interior pockets for your cell phone and keys, and water-resistant exterior fabric (sweat is wet!).

Tips for the Sporty Girl: If you aren't ready to fully commit to the sporty look, try incorporating just one or two items at a time, like a skater's zip-up hooded sweatshirt, or a cool pair of vintage track pants. If you don't already have pieces to use from your favorite athletic activity, try the sale rack at large sporting goods stores. It's often a good place to find gear you can wear on and off the courts. Look for items that offer a dual purpose like a lightweight cap or headband that has reflective artwork to keep you safe on late-night runs, but tames the hair during the day. Try hairstyles like the ponytail or messy bun—a Sporty Girl necessity to keep hair out of her face while focusing on her downward dog.

Body Type Alert: A muscular body shape isn't a prerequisite for wearing the sporty look. But just like any other style, the key is to show off your favorite assets, whether it's your long legs (with running shorts), your defined biceps (with a racer back tank), or your muscular calves (with cropped yoga pants). Certain sporty wardrobe features like the tank and athletic-style pants do have slight differences in styles that will work better for different body shapes. For example, when choosing a tank (a necessity in any Sporty Girl's wardrobe) your bust size will determine if you want a style with low support or mega support, plus details like removable cups in tank styles with a built-in bra or adjustable straps. With any style you choose, make sure your bust is covered while you run, jump, dance, skip, or hop. Athletic-inspired pant styles can include low rise, high rise, wide leg, or fitted, as long as you're comfortable and the fabric (try with a little stretch) can suit all your activities.

Other Famous Sporty Types

Michelle Rodríguez
Eliza Dushku
Venus Williams
Jessica Biel
Laila Ali

Case in Point: Serena Williams

In 1919, Suzanne Lenglen won Wimbledon in a knee-length dress with sleeves. Suffice it to say that things have changed since then. More than eight decades later, US Open champion Serena Williams hit the court in a skintight black catsuit. Serena's in-your-face fashion has landed her design deals at Puma and a fashion and jewelry line on the Home Shopping Network. Her tennis career has been hugely successful, but when she's done, it looks like she'll have a second career in fashion already waiting for her.

The Hip-Hopper
(for all the style samplers out there)

As hip-hop artist Nicki Minaj said, "You should never feel afraid to become a piece of art. It's exhilarating." And art is what's driving the modern hip-hop look. In the past, the style has ranged from athletic jerseys to baggy and sagging pants to oversized white tees, and today, artists like Pharrell Williams have capitalized on that style with their own fashion lines: Billionaire Boys Club and IceCream, which sell high-end graphic printed T-shirts and hoodies.

. . . .

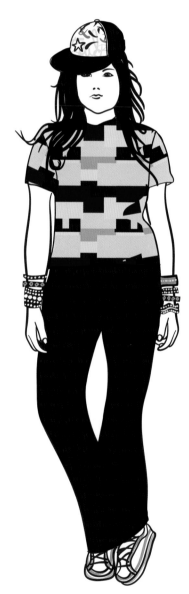

How to Make It Work: Think of sophisticated bright colors, wide-legged jeans, and of course, the shoes, which are so important to the look that some fans of hip-hop style even refer to themselves as sneakerheads, because of their love for creatively embellished—or even just really high-profile—footwear. For outerwear, every hip-hop wardrobe should include a graphic print hooded sweatshirt, or "hoodie." And if you can find a style with details like thumbholes to keep your sleeves down and also add ease to layering, or one with mesh venting to let out heat (while you're break dancing), consider it an added bonus. Other driving hip-hop styles include just about anything with a colorful printed design—best represented on tees, hats, and footwear. Big-name award-winning hip-hop artists like Jay-Z, Pharrell Williams, and Kanye West have also brought a polished, tailored side to hip-hop style with fitted suits and sweater vests (think Preppy meets Hipster). Pharrell owns the two previously mentioned clothing lines, Jay-Z launched the popular line Rocawear, and Kanye even debuted a couture clothing line at Paris Fashion Week.

Tips for the Hip-Hop Girl: Like the songs that hip-hop stars write, choose clothing that really stands out to you, and think of it as art you can wear. And if you can't afford that art, create your own. Purchase a pair of inexpensive plain white sneakers and think of them as your canvas. Use paint markers, which you can get at your local craft store, to customize your own sneakers at a fraction of the price (seriously, try it). Artist Amanda Yoakum's sneaker art—designs made from pieced-together bits of broken mirror and intricately painted scenes that take about a week to create—have been featured in art galleries and the *New York Times*, and sell for thousands of dollars. If you aren't quite ready to sport painted sneakers, play with other hip-hop style features like a cool graphic tee or hat. And don't be opposed to trying new denim colors like a gray, red, or even cobalt blue. Also, bright colors, big hair, and outspoken jewelry are key additions to any hip-hop wardrobe.

Body Type Alert: Hip-hop style can work with any body shape (more about specific shapes in Chapter 4), but pay special attention to the fit of your jeans. Gone are the days of sagging, low-riding styles—but don't sway too far toward the opposite end of the spectrum and attempt a tight, skinny jean. You'll know you've found a great jean when it fits comfortably at your waist and doesn't dip so far down in the back that your underwear hangs out (test this out by sitting on a stool).

Other Famous Hip-Hoppers

Rihanna
Kreayshawn
Missy Elliott
Lil' Kim
Eve

Case in Point: Nicki Minaj
For some, her outfits are more memorable than her music—which isn't a surprise when you consider that hip-hop star Nicki Minaj has strutted the red carpet wearing an ice cream cone necklace, a cartoon-print surgical mask, and angular, mirrored body coverings. She's also a lover of colorful graphic prints, Day-Glo makeup, and platinum wigs. This refreshing take on fashion has landed her in the front rows at major fashion runway shows (Carolina Herrera and Prabal Gurung, among others). Nicki is also bringing her sense of style to the masses—the hip-hop queen recently released her own line of candy-colored nail polish. (And why would we expect anything less?)

The Country Girl
(for life on the range)

At home in the great outdoors, the Country Girl has a comfortable-but-still-fashionable wardrobe that suits the relaxed, easy-going surroundings of life away from the big city. But before you start investing in boots and overalls, don't forget about all the garden parties and harvest festivals you'll have to attend, as well. The ideal Country Girl has a mixed-use wardrobe of simple at-home-on-the-farm-style pieces and more girly floral and fauna themed pieces. Haven't spent much time on a farm? Channel the farmerettes! The farmerettes were a group of more than 20,000 town and city women who, in the early 1900s, were brought to rural American areas to join the Woman's Land Army of America (which took over farm work after men were called to war). Most of the women had never worked on a farm before, but they rolled up their sleeves and in no time were plowing, driving tractors, and planting crops. And while looking chic at the same time!

. . . .

How to Make It Work: Unless you're really averse to the idea, you've got to have floral-patterned fabric in your collection. And when you do wear it, stick with one floral print at a time, unless you want to look like a disheveled bouquet. The number one rule for the Country Girl is to keep it simple and avoid too many accessories. Anytime you start adding layers of necklaces, handfuls of rings, or stacks of bangles, you'll automatically start to look less organic and natural. Stick to a mix of country classic materials including sheepskin, tweed, denim, and cottons with a soft floral color palette.

Tips for the Country Girl: The down-to-earth qualities of the Country Girl look make finding pieces relatively easy. You probably already have a denim jacket, simple tanks and tees, and a floral item or two in your closet. And in that case, your splurge piece could be something like a pair of great cowboy boots. If you do go looking for boots, stick with a more reasonably priced

Western wear supply store, which you can find in agricultural towns or online, instead of buying expensive designer reproductions. Your local vintage store is another place to look.

Body Type Alert: The wide variety of fashion choices make the Country Girl look a good fit on any body type—to learn more about shapes, sizes, and silhouettes check out Chapter 4. To embrace the country look, gals with broad shoulders or a heavier top-half should be especially careful when choosing any button front or zip front item (like a denim jacket, for instance). Make sure to purchase a size large enough to comfortably button or zip up (even if you don't intend to wear the jacket this way). By doing this, you'll be sure the denim won't fit too tight around your back or armpit area. If you are opting for jeans, make sure the length is long enough to accommodate your shoe style (heels need extra length and flats need less length). If you have recently had a growth spurt and your jeans appear to be ready for a flood (never a good look), tuck them into cowboy boots and no one will ever know.

Other Famous Country Girls

Rissi Palmer
Julianne Hough
Carrie Underwood
Gwyneth Paltrow
(at least sometimes)
Jewel

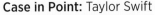

Case in Point: Taylor Swift

Taylor Swift's style is the perfect example of how a rugged country look can combine with the style of a southern belle. Her wardrobe, full of sundresses and cowboy boots, is the envy of millions, and many of her fans now imitate her country uniform (with curly hair and all), which Taylor loves! In an interview, Taylor said that looking out into the audience full of girls in sundresses and cowboy boots is one of her favorite experiences. The country music star, whose albums have sold millions of copies, and who's also one of the youngest people to ever win the Grammy for Album of the Year, has also signed a big cosmetics contract, has her own signature scent, and is the face of a famous denim line's advertising campaign.

The Bohemian (or Boho)
(for anyone who ever wanted to live in Paris)

Bohemians in the beat and hippie movements of the '50s and '60s embraced a funky, idealistic wardrobe that included a random mix of colors, patterns, and fabrics that mirrored the artistic and literary trends of the time. The term "bohemian" is still used today to describe the broad-minded, sometimes eclectic style of artists and writers, and the boho look is still going strong thanks to young Hollywood gals like Mary-Kate Olsen, who has a bank account worth millions but a wardrobe that looks like it could be found at a local thrift store. The former child actress has been credited with igniting the boho trend, and as a student at New York University, her style—which required a lot of work to look so effortless—was chronicled on a daily basis by paparazzi who snapped her every move.

How to Make It Work: Boho style should be easy. Don't over-think your attempts at layering or the pairing of the prints you choose. Think of key adjectives like earthy, airy, relaxed, and natural when choosing your silhouettes, fabrics, and colors. With these words in mind you will instinctively stay away from artificial and unnatural elements that don't function well in the boho look. Also, no outfit is complete without the right accessories, and that's especially true for any true Bohemian. A scarf can be worn loosely around the neck, tied as a belt, or wrapped around your tresses for an element of flair. Long necklaces can be triple-looped and worn as a bracelet, or double-looped and worn as a headpiece. Nothing's off the table here! But stick with natural materials like painted wood bracelets, delicate glass beads, oversized straw hats, and hand-embroidered purses. The fabrics you choose should also err on the natural side. Anything hand crocheted, woven, or made from materials like cotton and wool will generally be a good fit. Stay away from anything polyester.

Tips for the Boho Girl: The funky Boho's look is heavy on layers of oversized cable-knit sweaters, floppy hats, street-sweeping skirts, and too-big-for-your-face sunglasses. And with the variety of patterns, materials, and accessories available in the Boho's wardrobe, the style probably incorporates many items you already have in your closet, but which you may have never paired together. However, if a shopping trip is necessary, stick with thrift stores where the selection is already pretty eclectic and combines a variety of styles and eras. If you've never dressed boho before, it may take some getting used to. At first you may feel disheveled, a bit like an old frumpy lady, or stuck in some Woodstock time warp. To combat that distress, try incorporating a single boho piece into your wardrobe at a time—a crochet cardigan here, a floppy hat there.

Body Type Alert: Loose-fitting fabrics make boho style a harmonious fit on all body types. However, petite gals should stick to boho-inspired dresses and skirts that stop at least above the knee because a petite frame can drown in the combination of long hemlines and loose, airy fabric. If you want to show off your legs, try dark leggings (faux or real leather for extra points) and then pair with looser top layers. If it's cold enough, try a thick knit scarf and long, open-arm cape.

Other Famous Bohemians

Kate Hudson
Sienna Miller
Rachel Zoe
Mary-Kate Olson

Case in Point: Nicole Richie

Nicole Richie is a socialite, television personality, author, fashion designer, and (oh, yeah!) the daugher of '80s singer Lionel Richie. Called a perma-boho celeb by the *Los Angeles Times*, Nicole is often seen smiling for the cameras wearing bohemian outfits of flowing Missoni-print maxi dresses or breezy blouses, wide-brimmed fedoras and layers of cut offs, tights and boots. Her boho taste has made its way to her own '60s- and '70s-inspired jewelry line, with stacking bangles and thick cuffs that look like they came right out of her hippie-luxe closet. Nicole has taken her sense of style to television as a mentor on a new reality show, where she'll inspire other young designers to become the next big thing in fashion.

The Surfer Girl

(for girls who live their lives in an endless summer)

The popularity of surfer films like *Gidget* and *The Endless Summer* in the late '50s and '60s chronicled happy people frolicking on sun-drenched beaches, swathed in bikinis and board shorts—but you don't need to ride the waves to join in on surfer style. The laid-back look can incorporate beach-ready apparel while still capturing the sporty summer vibe surfers are known for.

How to Make It Work: Take a cue from the sea, sand, and sun when choosing colors and materials to incorporate into your Surfer Girl look. Opt for bright, scuba-inspired hues like yellow and turquoise, and make sure your clothing's fabric can stand up to the elements (leave the silk and polyester at home). Materials with moisture-wicking elements and water-resistant or waterproof properties (check the tag) are ideal in case you head directly from the classroom to the cove. For accessories, let seaside souvenirs direct your style with shell earrings, necklaces, and anklets. If you don't live near the ocean or plan to visit soon, create your own sea-worthy accessories. Most bead shops have shell beads already pierced with a hole, perfect for stringing up your own bracelet or other jewelry. Top the surfer look off with a tote bag to carry all your essentials—sunscreen included.

Tips for the Surfer Girl: Surfer style is anything but expensive. Surfers are known for spending their days on the sand, not in the boardroom. Their wardrobes are limited and lovingly worn to death (the more faded and fraying the better). So don't bother with designer reproductions of surfer wear. Shop for true pieces at your local thrift shop, seaside garage sales, and little surf boutique shacks (yes, those little stores on the side of the road that rent boards). You should also take another look at the everyday items in your closet. Using pieces you already own is the easiest way to create your own surfer look on the cheap. Jeans can be cut and then washed and dried to create your own frayed, laid-back shorts (just don't cut them too short because you only get one chance). And a sheer, oversized cover-up can be belted to create a flattering waistline, and worn over a onepiece for off-the-beach-appropriate wear.

If you have the crafty gene you can sew your own beads onto your cover-up or add thin strips of metallic ribbon on the bottom hemline to add sparkle in the sun—both additions are much cheaper options than buying an already embellished style. With the right outfit, all that's needed is a great pair of shades and some flip-flops (and maybe even a cute pedicure in a light neutral sand color) to complete the surfer look.

Body Type Alert: If you are lucky enough to take your surfer style to the water, don't fret over getting into a swimsuit. Designers are creating styles that fit and flatter any body type. Patterns, prints, and horizontal stripes can create curves. Wider straps can help support a fuller bust. And gals with wide hips can choose a style with detailing at the waist or the top of the suit to bring the eye up. Resort-worthy tunics work for just about any body type, but if you want to create more shape, belt at the waist with thin rope, a ribbon, or knit fabric remnants.

Other Famous Surfer Girls

Cameron Diaz
Malia Jones
Brooke Burke
Megan Abubo
Camila Alves

Case in Point: Kate Bosworth
Her role as a tanned queen of the waves in *Blue Crush* turned out to be prophetic for this beachy style icon. After learning how to surf for the movie role, the beach-blonde actress took up the sport in real life; she's even been quoted as saying that she tries to keep surfing as much as she can. Although she obviously can't sport a bikini on the red carpet, her off-duty style is still reliant on cut-off denim shorts, casual tees, graphic-print bathing suits, flip-flops, and sun hats. And her beachy hair waves are always ready to complement the look.

The Punk

(for rebels, iconoclasts, and mosh pit enthusiasts)

In the mid 1970s, the New York punk scene was alive and spitting, with bands like the Ramones thrashing around stages in leather jackets, T-shirts, and shaggy hair. And although the punk scene is characterized by its seemingly underground appeal, its popularity has spread to the front lines of fashion. The celebrated style magazine *French Vogue* has even showcased a 10-page spread dedicated to punk style.

How to Make It Work: In addition to tattered black-and-white basics, punk style also draws from a wide array of striking colors, eye-catching patterns, and generally loud clothing. To pull the look off, mix a brightly hued biker jacket (faux or real leather) with accented denim (think studs, grommets, or safety pins), and instead of fishnets, modernize the look with printed sheer tights in your favorite pattern or color. For a glam take on punk, mix elements like lace gloves, a velvet dress, or a satin blouse with harder-edge pieces like leather leggings, chunky chain strapped purses, and spiky metal cuff bracelets.

Tips for the Punk Girl: At its heart, punk is a do-it-yourself kind of style. You'll need to scour thrift stores, garage sales, and your parent's castoffs for the perfect pieces. If you haven't experimented with punk fashion before, parts of the bold look can be shocking to some. If your parents or boss aren't quick to approve, test the look out in batches—leather studded jacket one day, tangerine-hued tights the next. And before you go all-out with something as permanent as a mohawk, test out your creativity with temporary hair color in a shocking shade, a nail polish hue you would have never dared, or just amped-up eye shadow. Unless punk is your daily style, think twice before wearing the most in-your-face of your collection (dog collars included) to the more demure of life's little events—sister's wedding, brother's graduation from medical school, and grandma's 90th birthday.

Body Type Alert: The Glamour, Socialite, and Preppy wardrobes are all, let's face it, consumer-ready—meaning that if you walked into class dressed in any of those looks you may not turn heads. Punk style is the complete opposite. It gets noticed. It gets looks. And it will turn heads. To successfully pull off a look as adventurous as punk, you need to drip with confidence. If you're hesitant to show off particular areas of your frame, then don't. It's as simple as skipping the thigh-hugging tights and opting for jeans with a bit more coverage.

If your petite frame is getting swallowed by the hefty studded jacket you found at the local thrift store, skip it and stay warm with a punk classic: the red tartan plaid scarf. Punk fashion isn't synonymous with barely there styles more appropriate for the beach than a mosh pit, so experiment with layering options like vintage blazers (navy blue, burgundy, and hunter green are great color choices), zip-up hoodies (with safetypin embellishments), and even '80s-style leg warmers used as arm warmers (great thrift store find).

Other Famous Punks

Kathleen Hanna
Annabella Lwin
Brody Dalle
Joan Jett
Siouxsie Sioux

Case in Point: Vivienne Westwood
Influential British designer Vivienne Westwood (who received the prestigious Order of the British Empire award from Queen Elizabeth II), has been called the "mother of punk," and the Metropolitan Museum of Art has acknowledged others calling her "punk's creator." Along with her deep roots in the punk music scene, she's also been credited with reviving the corset and has managed to make punk fashion popular in the mainstream (even for those who don't consider a safety pin a fashion embellishment). As the *grand dame* of punk, Vivienne's fashion collections often include updates to the traditional prep-school uniform with the expected plaid and pinstripes, and the more eccentric elements like neon feathers. And Vivienne's feelings on political injustices are as in-your-face as her style. The flame-colored-hair designer used her fashion show credit sheets to support the cause (and innocence) of a fellow activist, and also used baby shirts to proclaim various political opinions and messages. (Oh, so punk rock.)

The Goth Girl
(for dark and stormy types)

Under a dark veil of chiffon and lace, gothic style makes for fearless style day and night. The look, which has its origins as far back as the 18th century, is still going as strong as ever. The Museum at the Fashion Institute of Technology has even shown an exhibition devoted entirely to gothic style in fashion, with designs by fashion icons like Alexander McQueen, Karl Lagerfeld, and Olivier Theyskens.

How to Make It Work: Goth style is generally pretty mono-chromatic (meaning that it usually only uses one color)—but don't feel obligated to dress head-to-toe in black. A charcoal-colored chiffon dress, midnight blue hair extensions, and a crimson velvet coat are all non-black options that can still be rocked as goth. Materials and textures aren't limited either, so try the softer side of gothic fashion with lace, off-the-shoulder ruffles, and silk. And if you aren't fully committed to the dark brooding colors of this style, incorporate a few lilac accents to lighten the mood. Opt for interesting blouse styles like a blood-red peplum top, which has a defined waist and a form-fitting silhouette with a peplum hem slightly flaring from the waist (think of this like a miniature skirt attached to the waist of a blouse). For your bottom half, try a sleek column skirt (and give everyone a glimpse of your sculpted calves peeking out through the outline of the fabric) with a hem that hits at the ankle and in a super body-hugging material like spandex, rayon, and Lycra blends.

Tips for the Goth Girl: If fashion character creativity was measured by height, Goth style would be a stiletto and every one else would fall somewhere between a kitten heel and flat. There is so much opportunity to use do-it-yourself skills like painting your own tights to create your own

own net shirt. Tip: Cut a hole, smaller than you think you need, in the area of the tights where the two legs meet and then pull over your head and use the former leg compartments for arm compartments. For more goth options (on a budget), scour flea markets for moody style accents like peacock and ostrich feathers (perfect as hair accessories). And don't be shy about hitting up the craft store either since it's a great place to find some lace and velvet fabric remnants (which you could use to make a choker-style necklace). Also the local drug store usually carries various brands of black, purple, or blue nail polish in the beauty department.

Body Type Alert: Goth style's dark colors are already flattering on any body type, but it's important to be careful with the exciting accents. Lace, feathers, ruffles, and other eye-catching additions to the Goth Girl's wardrobe naturally draw a person's eyes to the area where the accent is. If you don't want to play up certain areas of your body, then don't wear accents there (yes it's that easy). For example, if you prefer to play up your shoulders rather than your waist, stick with off-the-shoulder lace detailing instead of a chain-link belt (more on body shapes in Chapter 4). The tights (ripped, patterned, opaque, or sheer) can also present a problem for some. The brighter your tights, the more attention will be drawn to your legs. If you'd rather accentuate a different part of your body, stick with simple black or slate-colored tights, free from any rips.

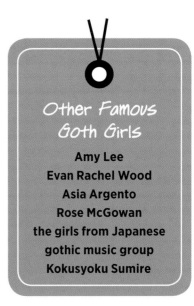

Other Famous Goth Girls

Amy Lee
Evan Rachel Wood
Asia Argento
Rose McGowan
the girls from Japanese
gothic music group
Kokusyoku Sumire

Case in Point: Taylor Momsen
Former *Gossip Girl* actress turned hard rock front-woman Taylor Momsen feels right at home in shredded tights, rock-band tees, and thigh-high leather boots. With a wardrobe of mostly vintage pieces that she modifies—in order to wear the same thing different ways—and a makeup routine that consists of the blackest eye shadow she can find, the gothic gal's style prowess has already landed her on the front cover of many fashion magazines, and she's now the face of an advertising campaign for a Galliano fragrance, as well.

The Grunge Girl
(for fans of flannel)

Grunge music helped put Seattle on the map in the 1990s, but since then it's become a vital element of American style all across the country. Although grunge was originally inspired by an idea of sloppy carelessness (which was made popular by classic '90s grunge bands like Nirvana and Garbage), it's also popular now in glossy fashion magazines and with celebs who embrace flannels, knit caps, and textured corduroy pants (think lumberjack chic). Don't stress if your musical knowledge ends at your mastery of the air guitar. Grunge fashion can also be embraced by people who aren't fans of the music. Fresh adaptation of the style often involves more color, and unexpected hues like yellow, red, teal, or orange.

How to Make It Work: Even if '90s music isn't your favorite, the new take on grunge fashion allows you to make use of a lot of staples you probably already have in your closet (or in the bottom of a drawer, just waiting to be recycled)—like a baby doll dress or a buttoned-up shirt, skinny jeans or corduroy combos, topped off with your varsity jacket, for instance. For accessories, avoid the bling and stick with simple homemade friendship bracelets, hemp necklaces, and suede handbags. And for an easy grunge hairdo, just slip on a cold-weather beanie hat to top off your ensemble.

Tips for the Grunge Girl: Grunge style should look effortless. Any piece of clothing that's worn, distressed, or faded can have a second life in your grunge wardrobe. To stay true to the look, avoid buying pricey new items and give second-hand clothing stores a spin for grunge-influenced staples. Your garage may also be a prime place to discover boxes of old winter ski clothes. The thermals, cozy caps, and plaid sweaters can help you rediscover grunge's glory days. Not completely sold on the plaid look? Try adding small pieces like a checkered headband, then move up to a flannel shirt tied at the waist, and finish with solid grunge cred in a cable-knit sweater draped over an open button-front tartan cotton shirt, low slung corduroys, and across the body suede messenger bag.

Body Type Alert: Don't be turned off from the narrowed fit popular with modern grunge style. The key is to wear clothing that can be layered, like cardigan sweaters, open blazers, striped leggings, tartan empire waist dresses, and basic long-sleeved tees. These items can provide coverage while still sticking to the slim look integral to the style (more about dressing for your body in Chapter 4). If your grunge style lacks shape (feels like you're swimming in a sea of plaid), add a leather (or faux leather) belt with silver grommet detailing at the waist. To add shape when layering, keep your final layer as a fitted one-button distressed blazer (distressed, gently worn, and even faded is key or else you will veer toward preppy). Layering doesn't always have to be loose and flowy. Keep the jacket buttoned over just a slim-fitting long tee, and accessorize with a scarf tied loosely at the neck.

Other Famous Grunge Girls

Kim Gordon
Juliette Lewis
Jenny Shimizu
Winona Ryder
Alice Dellal
Claire Danes (in her *My So-Called Life* days)

Case in Point: Courtney Love
The king of grunge style was Kurt Cobain, which only makes it fitting that his then-wife, Courtney Love, should be heralded as the queen. Courtney's been the front woman of the punk rock band Hole, and a female grunge icon, since the early '90s. And although she has been spotted on the red carpet in extreme moments of high glamour, her typical style consists of smudged eyeliner, baby doll dresses, and laser-cut leggings—*so* celebrity '90s grunge—which are all highlighted on her own personal style blog appropriately titled *What Courtney Wore Today.*

Fashion Action
Girl's Night In With a Themed Movie Night

Not ready to test out your new fashion persona in the real world? Host a dress-up movie night to get all your favorite pals in on the action and see just how well your new look goes over with a more forgiving crowd. If you want to sample the Country Girl look, rent a few Western movies to get in the mood. If you're leaning toward the Glamour Girl option, orient your movie night around a big red carpet awards show, or push play on *The Devil Wears Prada* to see how fashion insiders rock a glamorous look at work.

What you'll need:

- Invites
- Snacks
- Camera
- Fashion-themed movie
- At least one complete outfit

How to do it: For a successful Fashion Action, choose your fashion ambition first and then find an appropriate flick from this list that will help you to embrace it. Next, send out invites to your crew with a message about the intended dress code. Provide plenty of movie snacks and a camera to document your friends' stylish takes on your new fashion character.

FASHIONABLE FILMS

The movies have always provided style inspiration and fashion mojo for designers, stylists, artists, and other creative types. Check out some of these iconic films to see how influential movie style can really be.

Grey Gardens (1975)

The Maysles brothers' documentary (a cult classic) was recently remade with Drew Barrymore, but stick with the original for a look at Little Edie's real-life (and really unconventional) fashions.

Funny Face (1957)

Audrey Hepburn stars as a Greenwich Village bookshop clerk, with Fred Astaire starring alongside her as a fashion photographer looking for the next big trend. Real-life photographer Richard Avedon worked with director Stanley Donen to create one of the film's highlights: Hepburn posing for a fashion layout at various Paris locations.

Casablanca (1942)

Structured dresses, trench coats, and fedoras reign supreme in this romantic classic starring Humphrey Bogart and Ingrid Bergman.

A Hard Day's Night (1964)

This comedy, starring the Beatles, features a plethora of '60s style mod clothing and groovy prints.

Bill Cunningham New York (2010)

Bill Cunningham is a fashion photographer for the *New York Times*, and this incredible documentary shows how, with passion, a bike, and a camera (and very little else), he has managed to chronicle and influence the fashion world over his decades-long career.

CHAPTER 3

The Elements of Style

Now that you have a better idea of the look you want to achieve, it's time to learn more about the building blocks of styling. One way of thinking about these building blocks would be to imagine your closet. It's filled with dresses, jeans, and jackets of course, but it's also filled with reds, blues, stripes, polka dots, plaids—and a bunch of shoes, as well! These are powerful and dynamic styling tools, and knowing which patterns go together, which colors clash, and which shoes go best with your prom dress is only the beginning....

COLOR

Color is an integral element of styling. Pair the wrong color with your skin tone and you'll look pale (what stylists call "washed out"), or choose a color that isn't appropriate for the occasion—like Day-Glo pink at a formal wedding—and you'll definitely stick out (not in a good way). But used well, color can be a magic wand in your styling toolbox, providing just the right detail to grab people's attention and balance your overall look.

The Color Wheel

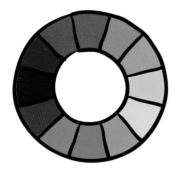

Have you ever been completely overwhelmed by all of the colors in your closet? When you're staring into a chaotic blend of royal blue blouses, tomato red skirts, grass green cardigans, and tangerine tanks, picking the right item from a sea of colors can make you feel more hopeless than happy. But thankfully, Sir Isaac Newton has a discovery that will help. The super scientist is credited with the creation of the first color wheel in 1666, after he discovered that pure white light actually contains an entire spectrum of colors.

The basic color wheel (which you may have used in an art class or seen at a craft store) has 12 colors that fall into three different categories: primary, secondary, and tertiary.

Primary Colors: red, yellow, and blue

Secondary Colors: orange, green, and purple. (These all result from mixing primary colors together.)

Tertiary Colors: yellow-orange, red-orange, red-violet, blue-green, and yellow-green. (These all result from mixing a primary color with the secondary color that comes next to it.)

So why is it so important to learn the technicalities of the color wheel? Well, wearing black is easy, but it's also pretty boring. With so many colors to choose from, it's important to at least know what your options are. But before you look like a Jackson Pollock painting gone wrong, you'll need to understand how color works. In moments of panic—like when you're stumped about which shoes to pair with your school bus–yellow sundress—a color wheel can come in very handy. Once you know how colors are created, you'll learn how to choose colors that work well together.

Analogous Colors: One of the easiest ways to use the color wheel is to simply take a base color and then choose an analogous color to pair with it. An analogous color is the one that sits happily next to another color on the wheel. For your yellow sundress, the analogous color would be orange or green. Problem solved!

Complementary Colors: If you're feeling adventurous, you may want to choose a complementary color scheme, which incorporates hues that sit directly opposite from one another on the color wheel. In the case of yellow, the complementary color would be purple.

Monochromatic Colors: Monochromatic colors are different shades of a single color, which can create a stunning look. Think of light, mid-tone, and dark shades. For a school bus–yellow sundress (a mid-tone shade), try pairing it with baby yellow flats (light) and yellow-gold jewelry (dark).

Triad Colors: For a bold and vibrant look, try a triad palette. Colors that are evenly spaced on the color wheel (in the shape of a triangle), are called triadic or triad colors. To incorporate this color theory with your yellow dress, you could pair an orange sweater and blue shoes to complete the look.

Color for Personality

Color has an aesthetic value for your style, but it can also have an affect on how you function. Researchers studying color psychology have found that hues can play a role in how we perform on tests, how creative we are, and how much we eat. If you want to play up the power of color, choose the right colors for what you want to accomplish.

Red: Want to improve your performance on the geometry midterm? Well, hit the books! But for a little extra help, why not give the color red a shot.

Research has revealed the color can make your work more accurate, give you better attention to detail, and improve your recall—just what you need to remember that pesky Pythagorean theorem.

Blue: Brainstorming topics for a kick-butt essay for your English class? Dress in as much blue as you can stand. Studies have shown blue gives people an edge on tests requiring imagination.

Yellow: Interested in adding curves? Scientists have discovered people eat more when exposed to the color yellow—in one study, the hue accounted for participants eating twice as much!

Color Blocking

For a bold take on color, try mixing colors to create a color blocking theme. If you've taken any art history classes, you may find the style reminiscent of the Dutch painter Mondrian. Color-blocking consists of a contrast of solid colors placed next to each other, in squares and rectangles of varying sizes. Designers have been inspired by color blocking since as early as 1965, when Yves Saint Laurent unveiled his famous Mondrian day dress with abstract and geometric patterns emblazoned in red, blue, yellow, white, and black.

But you don't have to have a designer budget to create the look yourself. Try color blocking with familiar color combinations in clean contrast. For example, well-known tri-color combinations like the patriotic red, white, and blue or the classic black, white, and red are a good starting point for newbies. With the three colors chosen, set aside one shade for each element of your three-piece outfit: So for instance you could wear red boy shorts, a white blouse (tucked in), and a fitted blue blazer. Done!

PRINTS

Prints, in any color, can be a stylist's best friend (or her worst enemy). But if you adhere to a few simple rules—and manage to disregard some big myths—you've got nothing to worry about. For example, contrary to what you may think, it isn't a sin to mix prints. Mismatched patterns can actually work really well if you stick with neutral or single-toned accessories. Dots and stripes play nicely, too. But as a rule, stick to patterns in the same color family. Here's a paint-by-numbers approach to prints.

Animal Prints

When it comes to animal prints, it doesn't matter which kind you choose— whether zebra, cheetah, leopard, tiger, or white-lipped python, all should be used sparingly. Generally speaking (every rule has an exception), animal prints should act as additions to a look instead of as the centerpiece. Use a touch of the print here and there to enhance a solid black dress, red blouse, or a tan pencil skirt.

Ikat Prints

The name may not ring any bells, but suffice it to say that you'll know an ikat print when you see one. It was created as a modern take on tie-dye, and the outcome is traditionally a diamond-shaped motif fused with abstract patterns. The handcrafted look of the print lends it to a relaxed, resort-wear vibe that goes well with maxi dresses, flowing peasant tops, and light scarves. As with the animal print, you should stick to one ikat print in your look, and don't mix and match—the pattern is strong enough that it should shine on its own.

Floral Prints

You don't have to channel Vincent van Gogh to rock a great floral print— although a few extra sunflowers never hurt anyone. Florals are one of the easiest prints to wear because there are so many levels of boldness. You can choose a soft earthly floral with a lot of pastels, a pumped-up microprint of tiny little roses, or a booming version with big splashes of oversized hydrangeas and pansies on a solid background. With so many options, floral prints can go from amazing to over-the-top pretty quickly. One way to avoid overdoing things is to break up the print with a jacket in a solid color (denim would work, for instance) or a broad belt.

Graphic Prints

Technology has had a big impact on graphic prints. Geometric patterns can be digitally transformed and given a 3-D treatment, and images in a picture or a painting can be blown up or shrunk down so that the original piece of art can be intentionally hard to make out. Graphic prints are almost always interesting, but they aren't always a slam dunk. The artistic creations are best used in short and sharp doses, so a sleeveless minidress with a graphic print usually fairs better than a print on a big, flowing dress.

FANCY FOOTWEAR

Your collection doesn't have to match that of Imelda Marcos (the former first lady of the Philippines who owned over 1,220 pairs of shoes) in order to give you options, but it's important to remember that shoes are a critical part of head-to-toe style. And although studies report that the average American woman has about 19 pairs in her closet, you really only need four pairs: a standout, a casual number, a pair of flats, and a great set of heels. At least one of those should work with any outfit you're likely to put together.

Have a Standout

Every girl should own one standout shoe in her wardrobe. It's the perfect over-the-top accessory to pair with an otherwise conservative outfit or to counteract the dreary winter. There are lots of ways for a shoe to stand out, but some obvious candidates for all-star status would include: tangerine vinyl flats, chunky magenta boots, or an ultra bright, color-blocked heel. A pumped-up shoe adds a wow factor to any look, but it looks especially great when it's part of a monochromatic ensemble.

Don't Ban the Casual Shoe

There's nothing worse than having your stilettos sink into a muddy lawn. You'll look ridiculous and you'll ruin the grass. No matter how dressed-up or dressed down your typical wardrobe is, you should always have a pair of flats or wedges that you can bust out for outdoor excursions, sporting events, errands, and any other scene where for one reason or another a heel just doesn't feel right. Find a pair in a color that goes well with almost anything, and above all else, make sure it's comfortable!

Flats and Heels

For both flats and heels, the fit of the pants is key. Neither flats nor sky-high heels will pair well with pants that don't fit, and the hem-length of your pants will sometimes determine the style of shoe you should choose. A flat that causes a dragging hemline can be a health hazard (don't trip!) and will eventually cause the hem to fray and become soiled. On the opposite end of the spectrum, the extra inches of a heel can sometimes make your pants appear too short, and leave you looking ready for a flood. What's an easy way to determine which shoe height is best? With the shoe on, the pant leg should sit at or above the ankle.

Style Icons: Christian Louboutin

His signature lacquered red soles have made cameo appearances in famous movies like *Sex and the City*, and have appeared on the feet of some of the world's biggest names (Lady Gaga, Jennifer Lopez, and more), but Christian Louboutin's shoes don't come cheap—some pairs have been known to carry four-figure price tags.

THE POWER OF THREE

Now that you've mastered the building blocks of fashion, you'll learn how to combine these elements with a styling trick called the Power of Three. Adhering to this styling concept can help you create a foolproof look with a minimum of stress.

It starts with a simple premise: You should always have three items in each wardrobe category (such as tops, bottoms, and shoes) that can be mixed together to complete a look. Then, after you've conquered the Power of Three, styling a flawless outfit at a moment's notice is no problem at all because all you have to do is make three simple choices from each Power of Three grouping!

The Power of Three: Tops

The three options you choose should work with a variety of weather possibilities appropriate to wherever you're living. For example, a long sleeve, short sleeve, and tank top would be good selections in areas with temperate climates. The top colors should also have similarities—for example, they could all be jewel-toned tops, or all neon-colored tops, or all pastel-colored tops.

The Power of Three: Bottoms

With your top picks for your upper body firmly in place, you're now ready to make some decisions about your bottoms. The three bottoms you choose should follow the same selection process as the tops. Choose styles that are appropriate for the weather—for instance, wool pants probably aren't the best choice if temperatures in your city generally reside in the triple digits. Clothing items can also be mixed, like a pair of pants and two skirts. Then, just like before, after you've picked the kinds of items you want, you'll have to choose the color palette. However, this time you'll need to make sure that the colors all work with the tops. Use the strategy you mastered in the color section of this chapter to determine which colors will play nicely with the tops you've already picked out.

The Power of Three: Shoes

At this point, all that's left are the shoes. Pairs of flats, boots (if you have a pair), and heels offer a good range, because they give you the most options no matter how short or long your pants are, and no matter how formal the outfit looks. For the color, once again, choose shades that will complement your top and bottom groupings.

Putting the Power of Three Together

When you're working with your Power of Three items, you'll just need to make one choice from each of the three subgroups: top-halves, bottom-halves, and shoes. That's it! With this system in place, instead of feeling overwhelmed from an entire wardrobe of options, you'll only need to make three easy choices. These simple picks will provide you with 27 outfit options (don't worry, we did the math). If you want to be majorly organized, you can even section your wardrobe into Power of Three groupings.

➡ *Fashion Action*
Make Your Own Styling Kit

Even the most inspired look needs the right tools to pull it all together. Professional stylists use what's called a styling kit when working on set or with clients, but every gal could benefit from a kit of her own. Think of a styling kit as a toolbox that has every basic resource that you would need to adjust clothing sizes, hold things in place, and create a perfectly polished look.

Some items in your styling kit are only helpful in *faking* the appearance of a great fit—but even those tools can still be useful in figuring out what you'd need for a more permanent solution. For example, a binder clip can tug an oversized prom dress into shape for pre-dance photos at your house, but it won't be as flattering on the dance floor. However, other items in your styling kit (like a safety pin) can easily hide a fallen hemline in your favorite pair of pants, or save the day in the case of a zipper malfunction.

BINDER CLIPS

What they are: These office supply staples come in a variety of sizes and are used to hold stacks of papers together.

How to use them: You'll be able to use the clips to tug and pinch baggy clothing into just the right fit.

Where to get them: Find them in desk drawers, office supply stores, and art shops.

Tip: Most stylists use these types of clips to gather clothing from behind. When the model is photographed in front, the camera won't see the clips holding the clothing in the back.

SAFETY PINS

What they are: This MacGyver-friendly tool is used to join items together and offers a quick and easy fix for all sorts of rips and tears.

How to use them: The multipurpose safety pin can be used to close a plunging neckline or fill in for a broken zipper or a missing button.

Where to get them: You can always go to your local drug store, but for unknown reasons, it seems safety pins are always floating around in desk drawers. The local dry cleaner is also a good place to get a couple free pins.

Tip: Be careful where you pin an item though; the hole may be small, but in sheer garments a safety pin hole can still be visible.

DOUBLE-SIDED TAPE

What it is: Double-sided tape offers all the benefits of normal tape with two times the sticky factor!

How to use it: Just because you aren't an expert seamstress doesn't mean you can't shorten a skirt or pair of pants. For one-night-only alterations, try using double-sided tape to create your own hemline.

Where to get some: Any drugstore or office supply store carries the stuff.

Tip: Keep in mind that double-sided tape is a temporary solution; it isn't meant to hold an item in place forever.

TRAVEL-SIZE SEWING KIT

What it is: A miniature version of the real thing, with a needle and a few different colors of thread.

How to use it: A portable sewing kit is ideal for fixing a loose button or creating your own hemline when you need more than a temporary solution.

Where to get one: You can pick up a mini sewing kit at most drug stores. But craft and fabric stores carry the items, too.

Tip: Mini kits can vary in their mini-ness. Choose one that's the right size for you, but still has a variety of thread colors available.

TISSUE PAPER

What it is: The stuff that adds pizzazz to gift bags.

How to use it: Have you ever tried on a dress with a neck opening that was slightly too tight, and wound up with your lipstick and face powder all over it? Try placing a piece of tissue paper on your face before pulling the clothing over your head. The paper will offer thin and unobtrusive protection.

Where to get it: Any place that sells wrapping paper, or in the "gift wrapping closet" common to most households.

Tip: Tissue paper works pretty well, until it doesn't. As soon it starts to rip or get holes, it's time to add a new sheet to your kit.

A CLEAN WHITE SOCK

What it is: Like scissors, you know what a sock is.

How to use it: Deodorant is a necessity for most, but the white residue it can leave on a little black dress is a very unpleasant side effect. Get rid of the residue by rubbing a clean white sock over the mark in tiny circles. It will remove the whiteness without leaving any extra bits behind (like a paper towel does).

Where to get it: Your sock drawer or under the couch.

Tip: Don't forget to wash the sock.

BLACK PERMANENT MARKERS

What they are: The name says it all.

How they can be used: You've probably already figured out this trick, but it's so valuable, we had to mention it here. A black marker is a great fill-in for black scuffed shoes, purses, and any other accessory.

Where to get them: Desk drawers and office supply stores.

Tip: Don't be tempted to use a marker on fabric that isn't a solid black (for instance, on a black-and-white striped shirt), as the ink can bleed.

LINT ROLLER

What it is: A handy little roller with adhesive tape that's used to remove just about anything from your clothing.

How to use it: Nothing says sloppy like a pile of dog and cat hair clinging to your pants. If you have pets (even the short-haired, hypoallergenic kind), make a few quick swipes of the lint roller part of your final prep.

Where to get one: Your dry cleaner may be able to give you one for free, or you can pick one up at your local supermarket or drug store.

Tip: The rollers work best when they have prime stickiness.

FINDING A HOME FOR YOUR SUPPLIES

Now that you have the supplies, it's time to gather them all in one place. You don't want your kit to start looking like an oversized hobo bag—a catchall for everything from receipts to packets of gum. Your kit should be well-organized and housed in its own container, and if possible, it should have at least a couple of separate sections, too.

Because we're really just talking about a basic container, there's probably no need to spend money on one. Chances are you already have access to some of the out-of-the-box options below, and if not, or if you want something more stylish or unique, reach out to neighbors, friends, and family. (I mean, why not? Just think of all the treasures lurking in Aunt Annie's attic!)

- Tackle Box
- Tool Box
- Shoe Box
- Jewelry Box
- Makeup Bag
- Messenger Bag
- Fanny Pack

CHAPTER 4

Understanding Your Body Type

Famous fashion designer Coco Chanel once said, "Fashion is architecture. It is a matter of proportions." And she's right: We all know the human body comes in an incredible variety of shapes and sizes, but sometimes it's hard to realize just how important your unique shape is to building and defining your look.

BODY SIZE

With their notoriously unreliable sizing practices, designers aren't making stylists' jobs any easier. This inconsistency problem is so widespread that some companies are now offering body-scanning services at malls to help customers figure out what size they are in different stores and brands.

And sure, it would be great if we could just look at a label and know right away if the item's going to fit or not, but unfortunately there isn't really a standard size that all designers use. Many designers rely on the size of a "fit model" to determine the measurements for all of their clothing. These models meet close to the exact measurements for that designer's sizing. So one designer's fit model could be slightly larger or smaller in certain areas than another fit model somewhere else.

The lack of standard sizing is also due to what's called "vanity sizing." Some shoppers are so hung up on size numbers that designers have started shrinking the numbers and enlarging the actual size of their clothing. Vanity sizing is more of a modern trend, so that's why if you score a great vintage frock, you'll probably need a significantly larger size than you typically wear.

So in the final analysis, the sad reality is that each designer or brand has its own interpretation of what measurements equate to what size number. Here's some advice: Forget all about the size, and concentrate instead on your body shape. For example, you and your best friend may both be a size 10 but have you noticed how certain dresses look better on her, and others are more flattering on you? That's probably because you're both sporting different body shapes.

BODY SHAPE

Choosing the right style for your body shape is one of the keys to achieving great style. Some style experts are really specific about body shapes, arguing there are as many as 12 super-specific types, but we'll stick with the five basic body shapes: the hourglass, the inverted triangle, the rectangle, the apple, and the pear. To determine your body shape from the list below, be honest (no one shape is better than any of the others!), and avoid choosing a shape based on what you'd want to have, or because it's the shape of your favorite celeb. Stand in the mirror with some form-fitting clothes, or in your favorite swimsuit, and compare the criteria of each shape with what your own fabulous body looks like.

A size 2 and a size 22 can still have the same body shape, so choosing clothing that flatters your body shape (enhancing certain areas and hiding others) is one of the easiest ways to feel more confident in the clothing you wear. When clothing fits well and embraces your body shape it doesn't matter if the size reads 4 or 14 because you'll feel confident and look beautiful.

Once you know what type of body shape you have, you can use that information to figure out which kinds of silhouettes will look best on you. Check out each of the classic body shapes in the pages ahead, and find the one that best matches your own. You'll discover the tips and tricks for shining in your shape, and you just may be surprised at a few of your famous predecessors!

The Hourglass

Some of the most beautiful women in history have had an hourglass body. Sophia Loren, Brigitte Bardot, and Marilyn Monroe all shared the trademark elements: a fuller bust and hips along with a smaller, tucked-in waist. The hourglass figure got its name because it really does look like an hourglass.

History of the Hourglass: The sumptuous hourglass silhouette was all the rage in the '50s, when Marilyn Monroe appeared in iconic films like *The Seven Year Itch* and *Some Like It Hot*. And up until the late '80s, the hourglass figure remained pretty popular, with busty, full-hipped models like Cindy Crawford dominating magazine covers, music videos, and runways. It wasn't until the '90s that the hourglass began to lose time (and media space) to waifish and rectangular models (think Kate Moss, whose rail-thin frame was plastered on a series of legendary—and controversial—Calvin Klein Jeans ads). In just the last few years, designers have begun to promote the curvy silhouette yet again, perhaps due in part to the success of the 1960s-themed television show *Mad Men*, where the curvy Christina Hendricks chews up her scenes in a variety of body-hugging dresses and pencil skirts.

How to Make It Work: Close-fitting styles offer the best compliment for all you Kim Kardashians out there. The hourglass body seems to be made for dresses, especially those that belt at the waist, but if you want a less risqué option, you should try a wrap dress. Wrap dresses appear to be one long panel of fabric, but when they're cross-wrapped around the body and tied in the front, side, or back, a V-neck is created, accentuating the waist and hips. And if the wrap dress provides a bit too much cleavage, just wear a solid color tank underneath the dress.

You can't go wrong with most dress styles, but definitely avoid empire cuts. With the empire cut, fabric flows out from just under the bra-line into a flowing, tent-like silhouette, which will leave you looking absolutely shapeless. The pencil skirt is a much more flattering option and it should be worn tight through the hips and tailored to end at the knee (no one-size-fits-all option, please), with a tucked-in blouse.

The Hourglass Challenge: For the hourglass girl, finding the perfect pair of jeans is like scoring front-row tickets for your favorite band from a radio call-in show—it's not impossible, but you definitely need a bit of luck and perseverance. Off-the-rack denim is more proportioned for a smaller waist-to-hip ratio, so here's the conundrum: If you find a style that fits your waist, it's often difficult to pull the pair up over your hips, and if you find a style that fits over your hips, there's usually too much extra room in the waist. To find the right fit, make sure that you can only fit your hand between your butt and the waistband. Look for styles specifically made for curvy gals (ask a sales associate at a department store to point out the brands), because a lot of jeans are actually created with more fabric in the hip area to accommodate the hourglass shape.

Other Famous Hourglass Bodies

Marilyn Monroe
Scarlett Johansson
Kim Kardashian
Salma Hayek

Case in Point: Kate Winslet
Kate Winslet's time on the *Titanic* may have made her famous, but her stance on plastic surgery (she refuses to go under the knife or get rid of her wrinkles as she ages) has turned her into a top-notch female role model. Kate has always embraced her curves, but her body-hugging looks really hit the big time at the Venice Film Festival, where she wore a headline-grabbing Stella McCartney frock. The tight-as-can-be-dress had a simple black outline running down the sides, which traced—literally— the shape of an hourglass. The dress became so popular, even trimmer gals like Liv Tyler were scooping up the style to get a little taste of Kate's curves.

The Inverted Triangle

Some of the most statuesque models lighting up today's catwalks sport the rare inverted triangle body. With characteristics like long, broad shoulders coupled with narrow hips and an equally narrow waist, the inverted triangle's name reflects just what it looks like: an upside-down triangle. Think of the shoulders as the long straight base, and the rest of the body tucking in toward the waist.

History of the Inverted Triangle: The inverted triangle is the rarest of all the body types, and its exoticism could account for its sudden popularity in the 1990s—the early days of the super-model era. That was when six of the most famous glamazons—Naomi Campbell, Linda Evangelista, Claudia Schiffer, Stephanie Seymour, and Christy Turlington—all looked down at the gallery from over high shoulders. Just as these models seemed ready to take over pop culture, however, celebrities stormed back to dominate magazine covers at the end of the '90s. In 1998, *Vogue*'s September issue (always their largest and most important fashion issue) featured Renée Zellweger (an actress with a petite rect-angle frame), instead of any of the inverted-triangle supermodels on the cover. It marked the end of an era. Nonetheless, recent inverted triangles like Gisele Bündchen, Karolina Kurkova, and Carmen Kass are bringing the body shape back.

How to Make It Work: For gals who want to balance their shoul-ders and hips, the key lies in finding items that appear to widen your bottom half—so look for full, flirty skirts that are fitted at the waist and flow out like a bell. If you want to show off your broad shoulders instead, stick with items that accentuate your upper half, like a strapless dress or a backless halter top. If you're busty, avoid items that are super tight around the thighs and legs. Pencil skirts, skinny jeans, and short-shorts can all leave you looking top-heavy.

The Inverted Triangle Challenge: The hourglass gal's body-hugging dress is the most challenging for the inverted triangle to pull off, but it doesn't mean you can't wear it. To widen the bottom half and create the illusion of a more proportioned shape, stick with close-fitting styles that have color blocking features: a solid color on top and horizontal lines or a patterned bottom half. New designs like the skirt-dress—a one-piece dress that looks like a skirt and a top worn together—will also help bring out those hidden curves.

Other Famous Inverted Triangle Bodies

Lucy Liu

Charlize Theron

Nicole Kidman

Case in Point: Naomi Campbell

Called the queen of the catwalk by *Vogue*, Naomi Campbell is no stranger to fashion. She was discovered while studying ballet in London and quickly rose to the top, getting paid five-figure sums to strut in shows for top designers like Valentino, Vivienne Westwood, Versace, and Alaïa (who even called her his muse). Her tall and lean shape, along with her total lack of self-consciousness, provided the perfect mix of attitude and appearance. And her popularity hasn't waned a bit. Even decades after she first took New York, Milan, and Paris by storm, she's still getting booked, starring in big advertising campaigns for Givenchy and rocking the occasional runway. When she isn't working the catwalk or the camera, she's showing off her broad shoulders and tiny waist in flattering pieces like the embroidered over-the-shoulder gown from Alexander McQueen that she wore to the royal wedding of Prince Albert II of Monaco and Princess Charlene of Monaco.

The Rectangle

Women with a rectangular body shape have bust, waist, and hip measurements that are all about the same. This body shape is often referred to as boyish, despite the fact that many of the most stunning and well-known actresses and female athletes sport rectangle bodies.

History of the Rectangle: The rectangle body shape is one of the most commonly featured (along with the pear shape) in fashion and pop culture. But in the media, the body shape had its first moment in the spotlight during the start of World War II when the US government had to recruit women to work in the war industries. To help, the government launched a propaganda campaign promoting the character of Rosie the Riveter (made famous on the "We Can Do It" posters during the 1940s). Rosie had a muscular and somewhat androgynous look (not overly feminine, like the hourglass, or masculine, like the broad shoulders of the inverted triangle).

How to Make It Work: The upright frame of the rectangle body type looks great in just jeans and fitted T-shirts, but to create curves, try an A-line skirt (fitted at the waist and flaring out through the hips) or a dress with an empire waist (fitted through the bust and flaring out through the stomach and legs). Both of these styles will create the illusion of curves. But remember, as a rule for any body shape: If the style is ultra-fitted (as in a bandage dress), then it's best to avoid things that are too short or that have a plunging neckline. Rectangle types should also stay away from generally loose-fitting styles like tunic tops, which will increase the sense of shapelessness.

The Rectangle Challenge: A figure-hugging sheath dress fits most rectangle shapes well, but it can leave a girl feeling curve-less. Sheath dresses often fall to mid-thigh or right above the knees, and like the rectangle shape, they have a narrow, upright silhouette. For a rectangle gal looking to add curves, sheath dresses can be a real challenge as a result—but they're not impossible. The key is to choose a sheath with a print, like polka dots or a floral, which will naturally add movement to the shape. Another option is to try belting the sheath at the smallest part of your waist to break up the vertical line. And if possible, wear sheaths that have embellishments like rhinestones at the neckline or a fringe at the hemline to draw the attention toward a specific area of your body and get away from that one, constant line.

Case in Point: Paris Hilton

Heiress, actress, and model Paris Hilton has the textbook rectangle body shape—long legs with relatively even proportions between her shoulders, waist, and hips. She works her look in styles like strapless springtime maxi dresses (perfect for barbeques!) and A-line spaghetti strap dresses like the one she wore to a designer fashion store opening. Both of these styles promote the idea of curves through the waist and hips. And when Paris does go out in figure-hugging looks, she chooses styles that still suggest a little something extra. At a viewing party for her reality television show, Paris drew raves in a pink, knee-length bandage dress with subtle horizontal lines (to create curves through the hips) and diagonal pink-and-white stripes through the bust.

Other Famous Rectangle Bodies

Cameron Diaz
Anne Hathaway
Serena Williams

The Apple

Thicker around the middle but with gorgeous broad shoulders and narrow thighs, apple bodies often benefit from items that bring the eye up from the midsection, like empire waist dresses. By combining interesting necklines or shoulder elements that draw the eye upward (think cap sleeves and sweetheart necklines) with colors that focus attention on your lean legs and arms, the apple shape can look as balanced as a beam.

History of the Apple: The apple gal has been idolized by some of the most famous artists throughout history, including Flemish painter Peter Paul Rubens. His oil painting from 1639, *The Three Graces*, shows three apple-shaped women as mythological goddesses. Some women have taken to calling themselves "Rubens" instead of apples to denote their body shape.

How to Make It Work: Apples are known for their great legs and shoulders, and look best in anything that either draws the eyes high up or far down (mid-thigh skirts with heels, or tops that have interesting necklines are always good options). Apples with larger busts or midsections should pay special attention to where the buttons close on a blouse. You'll want to make sure that all the buttons are easy to fasten, so that the fabric doesn't appear to be pulling; otherwise, you'll be drawing extra attention to your stomach. Similarly, any fabric over your stomach shouldn't be visibly tight or loose (so channel the story of Goldilocks and the Three Bears, and find a fit that's "just right"). Apple gals should also invest in a great-fitting bra. Not only will the right style make your bust look great, it may also help to keep any extra folds of skin from hanging over your bra line in the back (a tip that any body shape could benefit from).

The Apple Challenge: Apple bodies may look amazing in skinny jeans, strapless tops, and A-line dresses, but the jersey knit (the material used in wrap dresses) tends to be harder for them to pull off. Jersey knits naturally cling to the body, and the stomach isn't an area the apple gal wants to highlight. However, the wrap style in general is good for the apple; it's the often-used jersey material that brings a problem. To find the perfect medium, find a jersey material with extra weight (the fabrics come in different degrees of thicknesses), and grab a style that has front knot detailing. In a front knot, the ruching (a sewing technique) of the dress is used to create the appearance of a knot directly under the midsection of the bust, pulling fabric away from the stomach.

Other Famous Apple Bodies

Drew Barrymore
Tyra Banks
Oprah

Case in Point: Queen Latifah

She's a rapper, a well-respected dramatic actress, and an apple gal who knows how to play up her apple bod. She's often photographed wearing sweetheart and off-the-shoulder necklines that draw attention to her broad shoulders, collarbone area, and glowing skin. On the red carpet she tends to keep it simple, avoiding prints and sticking with tried and true solid colors. To round out her style, Queen Latifah is often seen with simple but eye-catching accessories, like a sheer wrap to complement a dress, or a lariat style necklace.

The Pear

Think you're a pear? Look around and you'll see you're not alone. The pear shape is one of the most common (and popular) body shapes for women. Pears have smaller top halves, with narrow shoulders and a small waist, while their bottom halves are larger, with hips often wider than the shoulders, and with the thighs and butt carrying most of the weight.

History of the Pear: Like their apple sisters, pear-shaped gals are larger in the legs, butt, and hips—but that doesn't necessarily mean they're overweight in those areas. Researchers have discovered that even if a pear-shaped gal were to lose weight, she'd still be a pear-shaped gal (just a smaller one), because she can't change the shape of her body. For pears, weight just happens to store in those areas rather than in the stomach (as it does with the apple gal).

How to Make It Work: Pear gals look best in swinging skirts and A-line dresses that don't cling to the hips. Pear body shapes should always enhance their upper halves with necklines that draw attention—so we're talking V-necks, boat necks, sweethearts, and cap sleeves. Gentle detailing around the neckline, and accessories like long chandelier earrings and oversized purses, can also draw attention to your assets. Ideal dress styles for the pear run the gamut from empire waists to wrap dresses that tie at the waist and then subtly flare out at the hips and thighs.

The Pear Challenge: The pear gal is lucky—she's got a great waist and petite upper body. However, a challenge for her wider hips and thighs can be finding shorts that fit and flatter. Stay away from Daisy Dukes, and instead stick with universally pleasing mid-thigh options. And if you're tall, definitely try a Bermuda-style short (the type that goes to the knee)—it's a dressier look and doesn't accentuate the upper thigh or hip area. However, shorter pear-shaped gals (or those with shorter legs) should stay away from knee-length shorts because they will appear to cut your legs in half (and the goal should always be to elongate the legs).

Case in Point: Kristin Davis
As Charlotte York in the hit show *Sex and the City*, the stunning brunette Kristin Davis was always impeccably styled (thanks to some professional help), but off camera she still knows how to work her body shape. Time and again she's been featured in magazine pages with flattering dresses and A-line skirts, and she's never without some embellishments that draw the eye toward her petite upper-body frame (think ruffles, halter tops. and off-the-shoulder styles).

Other Famous Pear Bodies

Jennifer Lopez
Sandra Bullock
Kelly Clarkson

COMPLEXIONS, COLORS, AND CLOTHES

Now that you have your shape firmly defined, and learned what types of clothing you should wear to enhance that shape, it's time to choose the right colors. There are things about you that are pretty hard to change (whether you want to or not)—like your body shape and your complexion—so in order to embrace these all-about-you features you'll need to learn how to utilize certain colors, that when placed just right, can make you totally shine.

Color and Body Shape

Have you ever walked into a room and been just completely wowed by a color—whether it's a cherry red wall, a bouquet of purple tulips, or a kelly green fern in the corner? That same eye-catching appeal can be used to enhance your best features and your favorite body parts.

The idea's pretty simple: The more pronounced (think bright, bold, and loud) a color is, the more attention it will draw to itself, while dark and neutral colors like black, brown, beige, tan, and crème will tend to de-emphasize the areas that they cover.

Hourglass: The curves of your hips provide a tucked-in waist that color can really help to accentuate. Try a dark, solid-color dress (black, brown, or navy blue) with a broad belt in a bright, contrasting color such as lipstick red or paper white.

Inverted Triangle: To balance your broad shoulders with your demure hips, wear bright colors from the waist down. A sunflower-yellow skirt would be a perfect match with almost any tank top (although the color wheel can offer further ideas on what might work best).

Rectangle: Color can help create curves for your rectangle shape body. Try thick horizontal lines in contrasting colors, and then add a solid black vest with a V-neck to create the illusion of shape.

Apple: Apple gals tend to have great legs. Draw the eyes there with brightly colored leggings (magenta, teal, or fuchsia) worn under a solid gray tunic or a navy blue wrap dress.

Pear: To draw the eyes up toward your best assets, use contrasting colors again. With black shorts, pants, or a skirt, a contrasting color (like white) will automatically draw the eye upward, like shining a spotlight right where you want people to look (say "cheese!").

Color For Your Complexion

Have you ever been told that a color looks great on you? Or has your mom told you that she "just can't wear" a certain color? Your complexion and underlying skin tone are what you have to consider when determining what are called your personal colors (which are just the hues that look especially good on you). Some people classify their personal colors in terms of the four seasonal colors—spring, summer, fall, or winter—but the two categories of warm and cool can be just as effective.

When you're wearing your personal colors, they should help to bring out the color in your hair, enhance the glow in your skin, and make your eyes stand out. But just as the right color can help your appearance, the wrong color can leave you looking exhausted, pale, and just plain unhealthy.

So in choosing your own colors, the first step is determining whether your complexion is naturally warm or naturally cool. To do this, take a look in the mirror without any makeup on. Open the blinds to let in lots of natural light, or bring a compact mirror outside. If possible, put your hair back, so that the color of your hair doesn't compete, and wear a plain, neutral top.

It doesn't matter what race you are or even if you're rocking a fresh spring break tan, the undertones of your skin color should still be visible, and generally fall into either the warm or cool category. Warm gals will have yellow, peach, or orange undertones, while cool gals will have pink, violet, or even light shades of blue.

Choosing clothing colors (and makeup) that are in your same personal color category should help to enhance your skin and generally flatter you.

Warm Personal Colors	**Cool Personal Colors**
Tangerine Orange	Snow White
Dark Chocolate Brown	Ocean Blue-Green
Creamy Ivory	Cotton Candy Pink
Field Yellow Green	Jet Black
Sunny Red-Orange	Lavender Purple

Color and Super Confidence

Colors can play a large role in your overall mood. Want to feel confident on that first date? Intense colors like orange and fuchsia can electrify an outfit and give you a renewed sense of confidence. Plus, unlike pastels, variations on these shades complement most complexions. Wear these colors as separates, so as a pair of skinny pants or a tank. But if you do embrace the hue as a full dress, or a total look, pair it with muted accessories like tan or gray shoes and a neutral belt.

Putting Your Best Foot (or Leg, or Neck) Forward

Have morning surf sessions left you with Cameron Diaz–style back and shoulder muscles? Or has your time on the track team given you super-toned legs? Everyone has got one body part they should be really proud of. If you're having trouble thinking of yours, ask a best friend for advice, and then feature it!

If you've got a great:

Neck: As you may have realized in the course of some famous slo-mo cinematic moments, there are few things more elegant than a refined neckline. So try a shirt dress; these lightweight dresses are based on simple designs and can be belted at the smallest part of your waist to flatter most body types.

Shoulders and back: If your silhouette is priceless, try a halter top. With a high neck and low back, your bare shoulders will steal the show.

Legs: Also known as wheels, gams, or stems, great legs make a serious statement—and they should be allowed to speak for themselves! So opt for anything that leaves them uncovered: like shorts, skirts, and dresses. If you have muscular legs (lucky!) stay away from skinny pants or leggings, which don't show off the great definition in your legs and may actually make them appear larger than they are.

LOOKING AHEAD

Everything you've learned in part I of this book has set the stage for Part II, where you'll start to develop your own unique style and apply it. With your body shape, assets, and personal colors now identified, you have all the ingredients you need to create a ton of amazing fashion recipes. Finding inspiration from your style muse, from the history of fashion, and from all of the celebrities, design stars, and style icons is a great start, but now you need to put your nose to the grindstone and get to styling!

➡ Fashion Action
Find your body shape muse

Now that you've determined your body shape, you need to find a muse to rely on for new ideas! Many photographers, designers, and artists have relied on muses to inspire their work—so much so that the Metropolitan Museum of Art unveiled *The Model as Muse: Embodying Fashion* in its annual spring exhibition one year. The exhibit focused on how certain muses (models in this case) shaped the world's definition of beauty.

To find your own muse, in your own body shape, just follow these three simple steps.

1

Make a list of three people who have similar body shapes to your own. We'll call these people your potential muses. This list can include anyone—your sister, your best friend, or a favorite celebrity. Just be sure the person has the same shape as you (although they don't necessarily need to be the same size).

2

Create a collage for each person with magazine cutouts, photographs, or your own drawings of your favorite items on these people. If your potential muse is a celebrity, do an internet search of the name to find recent looks that she's been photographed in, and choose only the best looks. If your potential muse is someone that you know, ask to peek in her closet and find the pieces of clothing that look best on her.

3

With your three collages done, ask yourself which one you're most drawn to. It could be a collage that also incorporates a specific style you prefer—such as surfer, glam, or preppy. Or perhaps it's a certain type of clothing you lean toward, such as dresses or jeans. Just be open, and if you like it, go with it!

The collage you choose will represent your body shape muse. You were drawn to this person for a reason. Use their sense of style and the clothing they wear to inspire items in your own wardrobe. And don't worry about subtlety here: Sometimes it's easiest to be very black and white (something looks good or it just doesn't). Not everything your muse wears will be a winner, but use their best looks to help you choose clothing that will look just as great on you!

Part II:
Style Gets Personal

Styling can be like magic, and now that you know the basic rules and have a sense of how to play up your best assets, you should have a bag full of tricks to call on when you get dressed every morning. (Think of yourself as a style magician who has the power to turn even junk into gold!)

But it's one thing to know what kind of a look you want, and it's another thing entirely to create that look in the real word. And while knowing what you want is an essential part of styling, creating your look is where the hard work comes into play. Building a wardrobe, constructing and deconstructing various pieces, and constantly (constantly!) editing your choices is what makes style happen in the real world. In Part II, you'll learn how to create a look that's as unique as you are.

CHAPTER 5

Curating Your Closet

Before you start styling yourself, you first need to take stock of what you already have. The best way to do this is to act as a curator of your closet. Curators—the people responsible for organizing all the artifacts that go on display in places like the Egyptian sarcophagi exhibit, or the award-winning collection of album art at the Rock and Roll Hall of Fame—have an uncanny ability to figure out what items a collection already has, which of those items work (and which ones don't), and where to find new material that really adds something to the collection.

Curatorial skills are absolutely necessary to take inventory of your style needs and acquire new "works," or pieces of clothing, that will complete your wardrobe and make your daily choices easier and more rewarding.

TAKING STOCK

A curator's first step is to research what she has on hand. Do you have nine pastel-print cotton dresses you say you'll wear every spring but never actually do? Or 11 versions of boot cut jeans you hang onto just in case you ever take up horseback riding? Or five little black dresses you've kept because they're all so different? You've got to start thinking like a curator. In a collection (your wardrobe), there's a limited amount of space (your closet) available for all your artifacts (your clothing). Each of the items that you're storing but not using is taking up valuable real estate, and it's time to establish some priorities!

FOR EVERY BLOUSE THERE IS A SEASON

Any good curator knows it's important to rotate exhibits. Do the same with your closet, and plan on cleaning it out as necessary. You know your closet best, but for those in warm or temperate climates it's a good idea to revisit your options about three times a year—once at the start of the school year, once at the start of the New Year, and once at the start of the summer. For areas with serious winters, like cities on the East Coast, two large cleanouts per year may be more appropriate—once in October to make room for the oversized puffy jackets and parkas, and once in April to usher in the warmer temperatures.

Whichever dates you choose, the annual clean-out will help make room for new items more appropriate to the upcoming season. Plan on spending more time (maybe even a couple nights) the first time you do a closet edit, while later in the year it may only take an afternoon.

THE FIRST SWEEP

Your wardrobe should be like a curator's special exhibit—a carefully edited group of items that are equal parts relevant and exciting. If you can't feel any excitement when you open your closet, then you're definitely ready for a cleanout. And don't worry: Editing your wardrobe just means you're choosing to feature some of your favorite pieces; it doesn't mean you're starting a fire sale. You shouldn't be haphazardly getting rid of items in your closet. (So before you toss that old beach cover-up, you should consider whether or not it could still work over leggings and a tank when you have plans to brunch with girlfriends.)

The real benefit to editing is that after you've made the tough decisions and created some space in your closet, you'll have a crystal clear vision of where the holes are in your wardrobe, and you'll be able to start filling them in!

Ready to start the first sweep? This is when you'll need to shut your bedroom door, because before you clean you have to make a mess, and it's a pretty safe bet that things are going to get scary. Your room will be as dysfunctional as an episode of reality TV, but the end result—a well-organized closet—will be worth it. During the first sweep you should place every piece of your clothing (and shoes!) into one of four piles: Give Away, Toss, Sell, or Keep, as described below.

Toss

This pile will likely be the smallest, as it should only include clothes that have something seriously wrong with them—holes that can't be easily mended or stains that have set up permanent residence. As soon as you're done creating this pile, bag up the items and look into recycling options in your area.

Give Away

Your give-away pile should consist mainly of items that are in good but not great condition and which are staples for daily wear—so stuff like T-shirts, pajamas, and old shoes that you no longer wear. You'll donate these items to a thrift store, where they'll gain a second life and also (if you figure out the right place to go) earn some money for a local charity. (More about thrift stores in Chapter 6.)

Sell

Everything in this pile should be in great condition, and to avoid having to haul clothes back and forth from a used-clothing store, you'll want to be honest with yourself about whether or not other people will be interested in paying for what you want to offload (so, for instance, trying to sell those pieces from a quirky trend three years ago probably isn't a good choice). The goal with this pile is to sell it at a consignment store, where clothing is resold at low prices, and where the money is split between you (the seller) and the consignment store owner. (More about consignment stores in Chapter 6.)

Keep

Don't worry if this pile starts out as your largest, because that's only natural. This pile will include all the items you actually want to keep—like that amazing studded belt you scored, or the jersey dress you got as a birthday gift—along with every item that doesn't fit into the Give Away, Toss, or Sell piles. But although the pile may start out the largest, we'll work on whittling it down to just the essentials.

Splitting the Space

Sharing closet space with a roommate or a sibling is about as fun as getting your braces tightened, but if it's got to be done, it's got to be done. Here are three tips for surviving a split.

1. Divide the space: Give each person exactly 50 percent of the closet. One person can set the dividing lines and the other person can choose which side she wants.
2. Never the twain shall meet: Once the sides are chosen, don't start letting your clothing items spill over to the other person's territory. If you don't have enough room on your side, you'll need to do a closet cleanout to create more space.
3. Co-op: If you've got the sharing gene (you'll know it if you've got it), consider having a space with items both of you can use: purses, belts, scarves, and jackets. Just make sure that you both agree on the specifics of the sharing arrangement in advance.

Pick a Pile

Sometimes it's hard to decide if an item should be in the Sell or the Keep pile. If this happens, ask yourself this question: If someone offered you money for the item, would you make the deal? If the answer is yes, place the item in the Sell pile and try and sell it at a price you feel comfortable with (we'll talk more about selling your clothing in Chapter 6). And if you can't sell it, you can always transfer it back to the Keep pile.

COVER YOUR FASHION BASES

After you've divided everything into the four separate piles, that's when the work really begins. With the Give Away, Toss, and Sell piles you'll be able to take immediate action (literally giving the items away, recycling them, or selling them at your local consignment store). Make a commitment to complete these steps within 72 hours, otherwise it might not ever get done.

Now, let's focus on your Keep pile. Choose your 10 favorite items from this pile and hang them back up in the closet. We'll consider this your safe list. These ten items are guaranteed protection, but everything else is fair game. Just like a curator creating a catalog of an entire collection, you'll now need to compile an inventory of the remaining wardrobe items so that you'll get a better sense of exactly how many items of each type of clothing you actually have.

Compare your inventory with the suggestions provided below. If your numbers are way out of whack, or if you already know intuitively that you have way too many clothes, consider transferring some of your items to the Give Away or Sell pile. That way, you'll make more room in your closet, make a bit of extra money, and add some focus to your collection (something that will help when you're getting dressed in the morning, too). That being said, if you want a few more pairs of jeans than is recommended, that's fine—as long as you've got a good reason for it (if, say, the jeans are in great condition, or you wear them all the time, or you're just not ready to part with them yet). You just want to make sure that everything in your closet is there for a reason.

Jeans

➡ **Why they're important:** Like peanut butter and jelly, the jeans-and-tee combo is timeless.

➡ **Amount you need:** The number of jeans you have in your closet should match the average number of times you wear jeans every week, but you should always have at least one pair.

➡ **If you can only have one:** Go with dark denim.

➡ **Popular with:** Hipsters, Tomboys, and Bohemians.

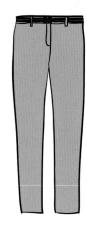

Dress Pants

➡ **Why they're important:** You should always have a dressier pair of pants available for an internship interview or for an after-school job.

➡ **Amount you need:** Three pairs.

➡ **If you can only have one:** Make it a solid color.

➡ **Popular with:** Preppies.

Blouses

➡ **Why they're important:** Blouses are perfect for "classing up an outfit" and making less dressy pants or skirts appropriate for interviews, dinners with friends, or a big date.

➡ **Amount you need:** At least four. Think about how often you wear one of these dressier tops in a typical month. If the answer's more than four, then keep however many you actually wear. For example, if you wore a dressy top six times last month, you should have six tops—but no more. If the number is below four, keep four tops—this should provide you with some variety without taking over your closet.

➡ **If you can only have one:** Choose a neutral.

➡ **Popular with:** Bohemians, Glamour Girls, and Socialites.

Casual Shorts and Skirts

➡ **Why they're important:** These casual basics are essential for kicking it with friends, hanging out at home, or just sitting pretty in class (as long as uniforms aren't mandatory).

➡ **Amount you need:** It varies. Think back to the last week of warm weather. Match the number of shorts and casual skirts with the number of times you wore those items during that week.

➡ **If you can only have one:** Choose a standout skirt, because casual jeans will act as the more basic pairing item. A standout skirt can be your stylish alternative.

➡ **Popular with:** Preppies, Glamour Girls, and Country Girls.

Dressy Dresses

➡ **Why they're important:** Dates, weddings, and school dances all call for something along these lines.

➡ **Amount you need:** Four—two little black dresses, one patterned dress, and one solid dress (in a color other than black).

→ **If you can only have one:** Stick with the LBD (little black dress).

→ **Popular with:** Glamour Girls and Socialites.

Casual Dresses

→ **Why they're important:** Casual dresses are an easy wardrobe choice (because then you don't even have to worry about matching a top and a bottom!), and can be worn in a variety of situations.

→ **Amount you need:** Four. Try and choose four dresses with different cuts and fabrics so that each one really stands apart. For example, if all of your dresses are cotton with spaghetti straps and floral prints, rethink your choices.

→ **If you can only have one:** Make it a solid cotton number.

→ **Popular with:** Surfers, Bohemians, and Country Girls.

T-Shirts

→ **Why they're important:** Sometimes the simple choice is the right choice.

> ### Making Space for Your Stuff
> If you don't have any room left in your closet, don't fret. You can create a lot of extra space with a few simple maneuvers.
> 1. Add a shoe rack below your hanging clothes. In addition to clearing up your heap of heels and adding some space, this will keep all your footwear organized and in one place.
> 2. Add a belt rack behind your closet door or on a wall in your closet. And don't limit the space to just belts—purses, hats, scarves, and necklaces can also share the space.
> 3. If your closet is wide enough, consider adding an extra dresser for clothes that would normally take up hanging space, like T-shirts.
> 4. Pay attention to the types of hangers you use. Most home goods stores and department stores sell hangers that are specially made to take up less room.
> 5. Remove winter coats. These and other bulky items take up way too much room in the closet. Place them on a coat rack in the garage, or in a long, shallow plastic bin under your bed.

→ **Amount you need:** About five. This is where there should be some serious movement. If you count the number of shirts you have in your wardrobe (don't forget about the ones in the dresser drawers!), you'll probably be shocked. T-shirts tend to be the de facto parting gift for your season on the soccer team or the charity half-marathon you competed last May. Most of these shirts end up as additional pajama parts. If that's the case, you should be fine having the same number of shirts as the average number of days in between laundry sessions.

→ **If you can only have one:** So much the better for you.

→ **Popular with:** Punks, Sporty Girls, Grunge Girls, and Tomboys.

Active Wear

⇨ **Why it's important:** It keeps you looking good while you're getting fit.

⇨ **Amount you need:** It depends. This is another tricky category where you really have to evaluate your lifestyle. If you sport (no pun intended) traditional exercise outfits in places outside of the gym—like walking the dog or running errands—you'll obviously want to hold on to more of these items than other people. So use the rule here: If it hasn't been worn in six months it's gotta go.

⇨ **If you can only have one:** Choose a simple black pants and tank combo.

⇨ **Popular with:** Sporty Girls.

Coats

⇨ **Why they're important:** Because when it's cold, it's *cold*! Enough said.

⇨ **Amount you need:** Varies by location. If you live in a warm climate you'll probably be fine with just one simple coat, but cold climate chicks have the option of at least five styles. (Otherwise winter can get boring in a hurry.)

⇨ **If you can only have one:** Hold onto that black pea coat for dear life.

⇨ **Popular with:** Preppies (and anyone who's constantly cranking up the heat!).

Shoes

⇨ **Why they're important:** You've got to protect your toes—so why not do it with style. Mary Jane, platform, espadrille, and gladiator shoes are fashionable choices that play nice with almost any outfit.

⇨ **Amount you need:** Four pairs—other than any special athletic shoes you may need (see page 62).

⇨ **If you can only have one:** Go big: Wear platforms.

⇨ **Popular with:** All flightless humans.

A Touch of Polka Dots

➡ **Why it's important:** It's just plain fun.

➡ **Amount you need:** One. (One polka-dotted item; not one polka dot.)

➡ **If you can only have one:** You've met your quota.

➡ **Popular with:** Preppies, Glamour Girls, Hipsters, and Socialites.

Something in a Leopard Print

➡ **Why it's important:** A little leopard print will add excitement to any outfit. Head-to-toe black can be accented with a leopard-print belt or heels, and if you can score a leopard-print coat, don't give it up.

➡ **Amount you need:** Three pieces—in the best-case scenario you'll have a blouse, an accessory, and a coat.

➡ **If you can only have one:** Choose a leopard-print accessory.

➡ **Popular with:** Goth Girls, Punks, Hipsters, Socialites, and Glamour Girls.

A-Line Shift

➡ **Why it's important:** The A-line shift is suited for any body type. The slight flair of the fabric at the waist accents the waist and minimizes the butt, hip, and thighs.

➡ **Amount you need:** Two—one solid and another in a patterned style.

➡ **If you can only have one:** Choose the solid.

➡ **Popular with:** Glamour Girls and Socialites.

Handbags

➡ **Why they're important:** Your keys, lip gloss, and wallet all have to go somewhere!

➡ **Amount you need:** Three—a satchel for casual days, a clutch for evenings, and a tote for carrying your books.

➡ **If you can only have one:** Go with the multipurpose satchel.

➡ **Popular with:** Anyone who has stuff.

READY FOR ANYTHING (AND EVERYTHING)

It's great to have a bunch of items that slot nicely into each and every aspect of your everyday life, but it's also important to remember those other, less regular (but no less important) events that still require a lot of style. So make sure that your Keep pile has at least one item that provides for each of the three key events mentioned below.

Job Interviews

➡ **Why you need the outfit:** First impressions are always important, but never more so than during a job interview, where you may only have a few minutes to prove you're better than your competition. Don't give your future boss any reason to doubt you or your judgment.

➡ **First choice:** A tailored suit with all the trimmings, along with heels and a tote (your version of the briefcase).

➡ **You can get away with:** A simple pair of dress pants and a nice blouse.

Weddings and Dances

➡ **Why you need the outfit:** There are some moments in life where you just can't get away with denim, and a wedding (or even a formal dance) is definitely one of them (well, unless the wedding is between two cowboys on a dude ranch).

➡ **First choice:** A dressy dress. But if you don't like dresses, stick with dressy pants—they'll do the same job.

➡ **You can get away with:** Anything other than jeans (unless explicitly indicated on the invite).

The 1950s

Style Through the Decades

In the 1950s America was free from wartime rations, and with the economy coming back to life, people had more money to spend. This new disposable income also led to fashion that was way more fun and frivolous than it had been in the previous decade. Small waists, colorful head-scarves, and full calf-grazing skirts in new synthetic fabrics like nylon, polyester, and acrylic were all very popular, as were designer fashions from up-and-comers like Christian Dior. As a result, closets all across America became a bit less dreary!

Meeting the Parents

➡ **Why you need the outfit:** When you finally get the green light to meet your significant other's parents, the last thing you want to do is start sweating about what you're going to wear. You need a fool- and parent-proof look that is sure to please even the most conservative 'rents.

➡ **First choice:** A simple wrap dress.

➡ **You can get away with:** Jeans and a blouse.

REORGANIZATION: THE CALM AFTER THE STORM

There isn't a lot you can do to alleviate the pain of having to essentially rebuild your closet. Rehanging and refolding everything that now sits on your floor isn't very entertaining, but it's got to get done. In fact, it's the most important part of the entire closet cleanout. So as soon as you've whittled down your Keep pile, put all of those essential items back into your closet. The best system for putting everything back in working order is to change the way you use your space.

Instead of treating it like a suitcase—that is, one large box to throw all your clothes in—make it work for your own particular lifestyle. If outerwear is a necessity in your winter wonderland, place your cardigans and coats toward the front, where you'll have the easiest access. And when you get to that old prom dress, place that one at the back. As you work through everything, try and incorporate some Power of Three groupings (the ones you did in Chapter 3), as well.

And now that you've made that room for new additions, Chapter 6 will tell you where to shop (and no, the list of must-have items won't include rhinestone-encrusted Christian Louboutins, because fashion has to be practical, too).

➡ *Fashion Action*
Clothes Swap

I've got a secret that I'll let you in on: You can fill your wardrobe with dresses and skirts and jeans and tees all without paying a single cent. All you have to do is host a party. Yes—a party; it's that easy. Except, to score an invite to this exclusive event, your guests have to bring items from their own closet—pieces in good condition that either don't fit anymore, or ones they're just sick of.

The process for the party is simple.

1. Choose a space big enough to host all of your guests, like your living room or your bedroom.

2. Ask each guest to bring at least five items of clothing.

3. Set the ground rules: Clothing has to be clean, in good condition, and free from any stains or holes.

4. Provide a "dressing room" for guests to try on clothes. This can be your bathroom, your closet, or another conveniently located area in your home that has some degree of privacy.

5. Once all your guests have arrived, give each the chance to show off her wares—holding up each item she brought so the crowd can ooh and ah.

6. Separate all items into separate piles based on size.

7. Let each person take a turn in choosing a piece of clothing. Consider the "take a penny leave a penny rule," and let guests choose as many items as they've brought to swap.

8. At the end of the swap if there are any pieces left over, you can donate those items to a local thrift shop. Everyone wins!

What you'll need:
- Clothing
- Invitations
- Snacks
- Recycled shopping bags or trash bags for guests to use so they can take their "new" clothes home.

CHAPTER 6

Adding to Your Collection

After you've done your closet cleanout and inventoried your collection, you'll probably notice a few holes. Perhaps you don't have as many jeans as you need, or maybe, after really analyzing the piles of shoes taking up valuable floor space, you'll realize that you don't have a single pair of flats. And special occasions like your sister's wedding or the homecoming dance may also require a little extra shopping. In this chapter we'll give you the lowdown on all of the available shopping options, and help you figure out where the best deals are, how to find that last essential item, and when to bite the bullet and just splurge.

THINGS YOU SHOULD SPLURGE ON

Pay attention here, because this is the one of the few times when you'll get a hall pass to spend a little extra money. The fact is, shopping on a budget has its limits: It's still necessary, on occasion, to spend a bit more of your budget than you normally would in order to get a few really crucial, high-quality items—like sunglasses that will protect your eyes—or items that are just about impossible to snag at a deal—like jeans that fit well and are in good condition. But this isn't carte blanche to put trend-driven, one-season only items (stiletto cage shoes, we're looking at you!) on your credit card. Stick with discount versions of those pieces. Style items that you *will* get the nod on include the following items.

Jeans: As mentioned above, jeans that fit well and are in good condition are often hard to come by for less than $25. Definitely try to find bargains (like on the sale rack at a big department store), but if you don't get lucky you shouldn't be afraid to pay a little more for a pair that really works.

➡ **Splurge on:** One dark denim pair.

Shoes: What's one of the hardest things to find on a budget? Shoes. Thrift store shoes are often too worn, and wearing shoes worn by someone else can mess up your feet (think foot fungus from wearing the shoes of someone who had athlete's foot). And discount shoes made with cheaper materials can sometimes cause blisters or just be too uncomfortable to wear.

Style Icon: Nan Kempner
The ultimate splurge shopper was Nan Kempner. Born to a wealthy San Francisco family, for 40 years the clotheshorse never missed a Yves Saint Laurent couture show. When the collector (as she's been referred to) died she owned more than 3,000 pieces, including 362 sweaters, 354 tailored jackets, and 106 bikinis.

➡️ **Splurge on:** One tan heel, which can be worn with both dark and light wardrobe pieces.

Underwear: If you've never invested in a great bra—one that you've actually been measured for and fits—then head straight to your favorite department store's lingerie section and purchase one. In many bigger cities, it's also worth looking around for a boutique that specializes in custom bras. The right fitting bra can make you appear slimmer, reduce unsightly bulges of extra skin, and make you feel more confident, too. Plus, they're just more comfortable!

➡️ **Splurge on:** One nude bra with removable straps, which can be worn with a variety of blouse styles.

Sunglasses: Don't mess with your eyes. Invest in a great pair of sunglasses that offer ultraviolet (UV) protection, as the radiation from the sun can damage parts of the eye. You'll usually want to buy sunglasses new, as the UV-protection details are found on the label, which will be missing from used pairs. Purchase sunglasses that block 99 or 100 percent of UV rays.

➡️ **Splurge on:** One classic pair that you really like, such as aviators or retro square frames. Then keep them scratch-free in a protective case.

SHOPPING: BUYING NEW

When adding to your collection, you've always got two basic choices: You can either buy new or you can buy used. Buying new is often (but not always!) more expensive, but it also affords you more choices when it comes to style, size, and color, and it can save you time. But don't make this decision a matter of policy; that is to say, don't just buy new or just buy used. There are advantages and disadvantages to each.

Department Stores

The first area you should head to when you arrive at a department store is the clearance rack. The bulk purchasing power of department stores allows them to not only purchase items at lower rates than boutiques, but it also lets them off-load some less popular (but not necessarily less fashionable!) items at huge discounts prices.

How to shop there: Get someone to help you. The advantage that department stores have over secondhand stores is that you can actually get assistance! A salesperson can inform you of when the next big sale is happening, and help you find clearance items in your size. Some department stores even offer dedicated personal shoppers for free. Remember, salespeople are just like you, and they have budgets, too. Be honest about how much you can spend so that the salesperson can give you tips on how to maximize your spending power.

The 1960s

Style Through the Decades

Style icons of the 1960s—like First Lady Jacqueline Kennedy Onassis—paved the way for exciting new twists on traditional fashions from American designers Halston and Oleg Cassini. The designers' full skirts (with impeccably tailored waists) emphasized hourglass figures in particular, and when paired with demure sweater sets and pearls, they created a now classic look.

➡ **Things to look for:** Take advantage of tailoring. Many department stores now offer free tailoring as long as you take advantage of the service when you're making your purchase. Depending on your body type, slashing this sometimes much-needed task from your shopping budget can save lots of money—and expand your range of options!

➡ **Things to avoid:** Be wary of purchasing an item that can't be returned. It might be thrilling to snag a neon green bandage dress on sale for $12, but once you get home, you may be left with the realization that it wasn't worth even the sale price. If you're going to spend a little bit more at a department store (as opposed to a secondhand store), you want to make sure that you can take your purchases back. Most department stores are return-friendly, but the policies vary, especially for sale items. Before making a purchase, understand exactly what the return policy is.

Boutiques

Boutiques are smaller and more focused in their selection of clothing than a department store. This makes it super important to shop at a boutique that aligns with your fashion style—whether it's an ocean-side beachwear shop, a posh city boutique, or even a mixed-use record store that stocks fresh finds for a hip-hop wardrobe.

How to shop there: Don't be afraid to ask for a deal. At big-name department stores, you'll probably never meet the owner, but at a boutique the owner often works alongside other salespeople. This gives you direct access to the person whose bottom line is affected by the sale, which will give you more opportunities to bargain. Start by inquiring about when the item will go on sale and then ask if there's any way to use your purchase power today for that same price. Sometimes, the owner would rather give a discount than completely lose out on making a sale.

➡ **Things to look for:** Seasonal items like coats for the winter or thin cotton dresses for the summer take up valuable space in a small boutique. Instead of impulsively buying these items the minute you see them, wait a few weeks until the season nears its end. At that point, most boutiques will start pushing the inventory toward the sale rack.

➡ **Things to avoid:** Boutiques are known for their stylish, trendy, and sometimes designer-heavy inventory. They also often have salespeople who are really great at their job and excited about fashion. So although you can certainly get some good ideas about new trends from the staff, be careful that you don't get caught up in the moment and spend your entire summer budget on a single trendy item just because the sales gal said you looked like a Katy Perry doppelgänger.

Online Vendors

Online shopping is the ultimate way to ensure that you're getting the best prices for new clothing. With a few keyboard strokes you can compare an item's price and availability across numerous sites. And it doesn't matter where you live: Even if the nearest stoplight is a 45-minute drive away, you can still take advantage of a great deal online. And even if you live around the corner from a mall, don't

More Online Shopping Tips

Have a question that can't be answered from staring at a computer screen (like what an item's true color or texture is)? Call the store's brick and mortar location, and talk to a salesperson there, or call the customer service line of the site and ask to be put in touch with someone who has access to the pieces. Knowing what you're really going to get before you buy it will definitely save you time, and it can save you money, too, if you have to pay for return shipping.

Also, subscribe to newsletters. Most online shopping sites have free eNewsletters you can sign up for. These email blasts often contain insider information about internet-only sales, free shipping promotions, and new merchandise.

overlook your favorite store's website since many stores offer exclusive deals online.

➡ **How to shop there:** Online deals can be great, but don't forget to factor shipping charges into your budget. Find out what the internet retailer charges for shipping before you spend hours foraging through the clearance section. If you're just buying one item, shipping can sometimes equal the purchase price. It's important to also find out what it costs to return an item. The best deals are often found at online shopping sites that offer free shipping both ways (for both purchases and returns).

➡ **Things to look for:** Only shop at reputable, well-known online stores. If you and your friends haven't heard of a site, ask around, and see if it's been reviewed anywhere online. You want to make sure you are only giving your or your parents' credit card information to reputable online sources since identity thieves can steal your personal information if it isn't properly secured—and the worst purchase is the one you didn't make in the first place.

Things to avoid: Don't purchase jeans online. One of the hardest things to get right with online shopping is fit, and jeans are the trickiest. The exception would be if you're purchasing a pair that you've owned before or tried on in an actual store. And if you're basing your purchase off a pair you already own, keep in mind how long you've owned the pair and how often you wear it. When you purchase a new pair in the same size as your much-loved pair, it may take a few wears and washes to achieve the same fit.

Begging, Borrowing, Stealing, and Styling

Using clothes from family and friends is the ultimate budget move because it's free! Take a look at some of these tried-and-true methods for restyling common household items for your own look.

1. Dad's tie: Use it to belt a dress at the waist, or tie it in your hair as a headband (party style!).
2. Brother's work shirt: Roll up the sleeves, unbutton a few buttons, belt at the waist, and add leggings for a new take on the tunic.
3. Mom's old clutch: To hide the look of a dated clutch (sorry, mom), wrap a brightly colored scarf around the clutch once, and then tie it in a bow. The clutch's old, dowdy appearance will now be supplemented (read: hidden) by the modern scarf.

THINGS YOU SHOULD SAVE ON

Even if you stumble over piles of cash in the morning and bathe in liquid gold, there are still some items that are just plain ridiculous to splurge on. Sometimes this is because a particular item is just too easy to get for cheap, or because no one could ever tell the difference between the expensive version and the budget version. But whatever the case may be, saving on key pieces in your closet can give your wallet a little breathing room, and give you a little more peace of mind. Here are some style items that need to get the budget treatment.

➡ **Leggings:** Department stores do sell expensive designer leggings, but stay away from these, and instead purchase thick black panty-hose at a drugstore or a supermarket (stay away from anything sheer). They're just a few dollars and they provide a great (and easy) imitation of the expensive look.

➡ **Jewelry:** Sure, that diamond brooch is probably out of your budget, but there are plenty of clothing chains that offer great deals on reproductions that are made with cheaper materials to look like the expensive stuff.

➡ **Scarves:** As a wallet-friendly, lightweight, and adaptable fashion accessory that adds color or texture to a look, scarves are a great purchase. Look for well-priced scarves at department store outlets, budget clothing chains, and in areas like the belt rack and purse section at consignment, resale, and thrift shops.

SHOPPING: BUYING USED

Few things are as thrilling as finding clothing that fits and flatters—especially when it's wallet-friendly, too. This is especially true for young fashionistas who are on a tight budget (sound familiar?). As far as a bottom-line price, it doesn't get much better than the world of second-hand clothing.

Thrift Stores

Thrift stores are secondhand shops where donated clothing is resold at low prices, often to benefit an organization. Stylistically, thrift stores aren't exactly Neiman Marcus or Saks Fifth Avenue, but clothes that were purchased at those high-end department stores sometimes end up there. You'll want to check your uptight tendencies at the door, because thrift stores can be as disorganized as your locker during finals week. Still, it's worth wading through the mess, because a thrift store is the perfect place to create an entire look for pennies on the dollar.

⇨ **How to shop there:** Go in with an agenda, and be prepared to spend a fair amount of time there. At thrift stores, there usually aren't many salespeople to help you scour the racks for the perfect pencil skirt, or even help you find your size. You're going to have to do the investigative work yourself. Having an agenda can help you manage your time better. Have a clear vision of the look you're trying to create and then enter the store with the key pieces already in mind. Thrift stores often have specific sections for each type of clothing (jeans, sweaters, dresses, etc.), and with definitive items on your agenda you can head directly to the most relevant areas of the store.

⇨ **Things to look for:** As a general rule, thrift stores are great for buying basics such as casual T-shirts, denim items, and layering pieces like cardigans. If you're lucky, you might even find a prized possession like a trendy wrap dress—but designer items often get pulled off the racks by the thrift store staff, or purchased by professional stylists or consignment store owners. However, that doesn't mean you won't score a few gently loved name-brand pieces at a fraction of the price. It all comes down to timing, luck, and perseverance.

⇨ **Things to avoid:** Be on the lookout for armpit stains, holes, and shrinkage from repeated washings. It's rarely worth it to repair items with significant damage. And remember: If an item seems too good to be true, it probably is.

Consignment Stores

The consignment store is like the more refined big sister of the thrift shop. Whereas people donate clothes to a thrift store (and get nothing in return except a tax write-off), people bring in old (but nice) clothes to a consignment store, and then leave them there on loan in hopes that the store can sell them and give them a cut. Because most stores carry only name-brand pieces, and two people (the seller and the store owner) need to recoup a profit on the piece, the deals here aren't as great as the ones at thrift shops. But it's a smart way to get designer duds for about half the price of what they cost new.

⇒ **How to shop there:** Think before you buy. Just because there are deals to be had doesn't mean you should always take them. Most consignment stores have a "No" policy: No returns, no exchanges, and no store credit. When confronted with a can't-pass-it-up kind of deal, ask yourself how many times, realistically speaking, you'll be able to wear the item this month. If a gorgeous cashmere sweater is going to sit in your closet because your town is still nine months away from cold weather, it may not be worth making the investment now. By the time you could wear the piece you might not fit in it or your style and taste could change.

⇒ **Things to look for:**

Look for consignment stores that match your style. When you're ready to start shopping try and choose a neighborhood that is representative of the look you want to create. The stock at consignment stores varies dramatically based on who sells their clothing there, which in turn has a lot to do with who lives (or works) nearby. So if you're looking for fancy stuff, you might want to shop in a swanky uptown neighborhood, and if you're in the mood for fashion-forward and trend-driven pieces, stick to the almost-always hip downtown neighborhoods.

> **Sell Your Own Stuff**
>
> If you want to make extra money—or even just make some extra room in your closet—try selling your clothes at a consignment store. Here are five tips to get the sale.
>
> 1. Make an appointment or find out the appropriate time to show your items.
> 2. Make sure your clothing is clean.
> 3. Iron or steam the clothing before selling it so it appears in its best condition.
> 4. Wait to sell seasonal clothing like a thick winter coat until a few weeks before the season approaches.
> 5. Don't show up with garbage bags of clothing. Bring the clothing on hangers or nicely folded in a suitcase.

⇒ **Things to avoid:** Just because an item is at a consignment store doesn't automatically make it a good deal. If it doesn't fit or you won't get much use out of it, don't buy it—no matter how cheap the price seems. Just like at a retail store, you also want to avoid paying full price. Most consignment stores put things on sale when they don't sell at the first price. The reason stores are willing to do this is because there was no original investment made to purchase the piece (the seller just loaned it to them), and they want to move things out of the store to allow space for new clothing to come in. If you've found your dream item but it isn't on sale, take a shot and ask an employee how long the piece has been available and when the price is expected to come down. If the date is near, you'll sometimes find the store owner or manager will be willing to give you the discount.

CONCLUSION

Shopping is a complicated art form, and wherever and however you're hunting for deals, there's almost always something that you could be doing better (or getting for cheaper). But in general, if you stay true to your budget, keep your eyes open, remain honest with yourself, and don't just shop to shop, you should be able to keep regrets to a minimum. Choose items with the careful eye of a stylist, and make sure each purchase is really necessary and fills a hole in your wardrobe.

➡ *Fashion Action*
Build a Look for Less

Do you think you've mastered the art of budget shopping? Test out your new skills by building a complete look for less. The challenge is to pull together a stylish, ready-to-wear outfit while only "spending" (this can be real dollars or imagined money) $10, $30, or $50. If you can do it in under $10, consider yourself on the Varsity Budget Team; if it takes $30, you're rocking the JV Budget Team, and if you need $50, well, you may have made the team, but you'll be spending a lot of time on the bench until you learn to trim your tastes. Better luck next year!

DETAILS

1. Find an inspiration for your look. It could be an outfit that was worn by your favorite actress, a recent vacation you took, or even an era in time. Your mood board may be a good spot to turn to for inspiration.

2. Think about the kind of place you'd wear this look. Are you looking for an outfit for a school dance? Something to wear to a party? A casual weekend look?

3. Use at least three different resources to find the items that will create your complete look. If you don't want to spend real money you can cut images out of magazines or a fashion catalog, print out items you find for sale at an online retailer, or take pictures of your favorite clothes at a retail store or thrift shop. Just remember to keep track of how much each item would cost if you were spending real money.

4. Look in your closet to see if you can incorporate an item you already own into your new budget look—but limit yourself to only one item. Part of building a look is utilizing both what you've already got and what you still need to find.

5. Constantly check your budget. After each item you've added, calculate your new total so you'll know what's left to spend. If your total look isn't within your budget, swap things out until you get it right. Take a look back at the "Things You Should Save On" section in this chapter for other inspirations for more budget-friendly pieces.

CHAPTER 7

Putting Everything Together Like a Pro

Once you know what you already have in your wardrobe, along what you still need and what you still want, you can start to actually put some looks together. This chapter will show you just how easy it can be to pull together a perfectly coordinated outfit from seemingly stale separates, and offer some ideas about how you can pick the right materials for the right occasion, all while accessorizing with ease. You'll learn how to sidestep amateur fashion mistakes—like wearing the same pair of jeans with both your too-tall stilettos and your fab flats—and start to make the transition into a true stylist.

CREATING A LOOK FROM HEAD TO TOE

You've learned all about the theories of color selection and dressing for your body shape in previous chapters, but this is the chapter where you'll learn how to create a look from head to toe. Because sure, fashion is personal and fashion is fluid, but there are a lot of little tools and tricks that can help keep you from accidentally looking like a circus tent or a sack of potatoes in your new, dynamic outfits. No solution is universal, and every rule has an exception, but a basic, everyday checklist can help ensure that you don't ever hit an unfortunate extreme.

The Rules You Need

Even if as a rule you like to play it safe, understand that at some point you will still make a fashion mistake. You will create an outfit that has a slight flaw (too many accessories!), a minor weakness (head-to-toe faded black!), or one that just doesn't work anymore (tights as pants three years down the road, for instance). This is because fashion is an evolution. Your taste and your mastery of styling will continue to grow—one of the reasons most of us cringe at the outfits we were wearing in last year's photos. To ensure that your stumbles don't outnumber your successes, you can raise your super style quotient by following a few simple fashion rules.

Rule 1: Dump the Bogus Color Rules: Have you ever heard someone say, "Don't wear white after Labor Day"? There are a lot of outdated color rules like this that are best left alone! Even the queen of etiquette, Emily Post, agrees that you should embrace your winter whites and rock the color well after the first days of September. And the idea that black and brown can't be worn together—it's so not true! Just choose a dark chocolate brown and pair it with a contrasting jet-black piece. For example, try a brown button-up trench coat and black trousers or brown leather boots with black tights—*Project Runway*'s Tim Gunn has said few other looks are quite as chic.

Rule 2: Barer Beware: Don't make the mistake of doing too much with too little (when it comes to clothes at least)! As a rule, going bare in more than one area at once just doesn't work. You may like to show off your great legs, your back, and your broad shoulders, but choose only one feature to focus on at a time. Strapless and backless tops shouldn't be matched with mini-skirts, but they can look great with a fitted pencil-style skirt. And a fantastic body-hugging dress that falls inches above the knee definitely looks stylish with off-the-shoulder long sleeves. But don't convince yourself that wearing tights with a short skirt will override this rule—or that starting out the night with a cardigan (which you'll take off immediately when you enter the room) will counteract the strapless-mini combo.

Rule 3: Accessor-Three: Repeat these words: "I am not a Christmas tree." You've probably seen the head-to-toe bauble look, when a girl wears every ring she owns, along with a three-strand beaded necklace, dangling drop earrings, a long feather tied in her hair, an oversized men's watch, and a toe ring, too. It's way too much. With so many accessories, she starts to resemble a Christmas tree loaded down with ornaments. As a rule, don't include more than three accessories at any one time. You can choose any three accessories you'd like: Earrings, bracelet, and headband—check—or anklet, cuff, and chandelier earrings—sounds great. But stop after that.

Rule 4: Mind the Materials: There are some materials that are just better suited for certain occasions, or even for certain times of day. For example, fabric that is shimmery and iridescent should only be worn at night (unless you're walking the red carpet during an afternoon awards gala). On the other hand, clothing in a more casual fabric like a cotton knit is better suited for an alfresco lunch

Marvelous Mani

There are some women who change their polish color each night, carefully coordinating the hue with their look for the next day. You can save a lot of time and get equally stylish results by choosing a color that is universally flattering (sorry, not your spring break neon green) like a sheer pink, a beige hue that has a slight golden undertone, or a deep burgundy. These classic shades will pair nicely with any skin tone and won't clash with your ensemble.

than a charity dinner under the stars. If you're prone to sweating, you should also pay special attention to the materials your clothing is made from. As a rule, stay away from fabrics that don't breathe such as polyester, corduroy, and acetate. When a fabric breathes (like 100 percent cotton and linen), it carries moisture from one side to the other instead of trapping the sweat inside (stink factor: high).

Rule 5: Cool it on the Casuals: There are few circumstances where a long gown is appropriate for casual wear. When a dress is long, it's often associated with sundown attire. It's why you'll wear a short A-line dress to your cousin's wedding brunch instead of a taffeta ball gown. With that in mind, in certain situations, casual wear has gotten a bit too casual. When styling, it's important that you (or your client) looks appropriate for the setting. Wearing your yoga pants anywhere besides the gym and your house isn't a good choice (grocery shopping excluded). Put a little effort into even your most casual look. As a rule, a cute blouse, when tucked into your favorite shorts and paired with an over-the-shoulder handbag is an easy but casually fashionable look.

Common Styling Mistakes

Professional stylists aren't immune from styling mistakes. Chances are, if you study the photo shoots that you see in your favorite fashion magazines, you'll be able to catch a few of the common blunders listed below. The key is to know what the mistakes are so that you watch out for them before they happen. Then, if you ever become a professional stylist, it will save you lots of time begging the art director to retouch your boo-boo.

Shoes that Don't Fit: Whenever photos are going to be taken of you or your client, you have to be particularly careful when working with open-toe or heel-exposing shoes. There's nothing worse than an otherwise great looking photo where the model's foot is left hanging off the shoe, or swimming in a too-large pair. In real life, the only fix is to find a pair that is actually the right size—but in cases of emergency there are a few tricks to make the shoe appear to fit.

If the model's foot is too small: For a closed-toe shoe, have the model bring her heel to the back of the shoe during the shot. For an open-toe style, have her position her foot so that it's only being photographed from the front.

If the model's foot is too large: For an open-heel style, makes sure the shoe is only shot from the front, so the camera doesn't capture her heel hanging off the edge of the shoe. For a closed-toe shoe—well, there you're out of luck (unless you happen to have a shrink-ray gun on hand).

For a real-life fix, ditch any shoes that are too small—you'll just end up hurting your feet. For shoes that are too big, double up on your socks if socks are appropriate (with boots, for instance), or invest in a pair of thick ski socks (from a sporting goods store). The trick will probably get your foot to work in shoes that are up to a size too large.

The 1970s and 1980s

Style Through the Decades

It was only a few decades ago that metallic hot pants and bell-bottom trousers (the bigger the better) dominated the 1970s. The 1980s—never a decade to be outdone—followed it up with acid-wash denim jeans, spandex one-piece body suits, and neon leg warmers. And although designers love to resurrect trends of the past, the true, original takes on these styles have been relegated to the Halloween costume pile. And let that be a lesson to us all: The items we love now just may become their own styling mistake in the future. When you're trying to bring any decades-old fashion back in style, the trick is to keep the spirit of the original through a more modest (read: less spandexy) update.

Jewelry That Doesn't Fit: As a stylist, you also have to pay particular attention to the size of your client (or yourself) when using jewelry in your look. Fingers, necks, and wrists come in a variety of sizes. You can't just assume that the jewelry you *want* to use is the jewelry you *can* use. For example, a necklace that's perfectly positioned above the collarbone on one woman could be a choker on another. A metal watch may need to have links taken out to fit the petite wrist of a client. And rings are often the toughest. When working with a model it's hard to guess her ring size. If you end up on location and the ring is obviously too big, ensure that the gap between the ring and the finger isn't visible in the shot. Tell the model to keep her fingers together or have the front of the hand facing the camera. For a real-life fix, consider wearing the cool (but oversized ring) on a chain and sporting it as a necklace. You'll still get to show off the accessory but you won't have to worry about it falling off.

Swimming in a Sea of Fabric: The fit of the clothing should be the first thing a stylist considers, but all too often it's the fit that ends up ruining an otherwise perfect look. There are plenty of women walking down the street in coats that are so big you wonder if they're wrapped up in a king-sized comforter. In a perfect world we'd all have tailors, but in real life the best way to avoid this mistake is to only purchase clothing that fits when you buy it, and that you get rid of when the buttons start to pop. That way you won't be tempted to bust out the trench coat you haven't worn for three seasons and two growth spurts.

On camera, it's a different story: You'll always be able to recreate the look of a fitted garment with the aid of safety pins. Always pin from the back and start with small sections of fabric. If you're borrowing the look, be careful not to rip any delicate fabric. If you're concerned, ditch the safety pins and stick with clothing pins. Point out to the photographer where the pins are located and make sure that the model isn't angling her body in a way that will allow the camera to catch the pins.

You're Ready for the Flood: We all have that favorite pair of jeans. The color is just right, the distressed areas are in the perfect locations, and the subtle detailing on the pockets is perfect. But loving a pair of jeans so much that you can't admit you're too tall to rock them is a big fashion no-no. As a rule, if your anklebone is visible outside of your jeans, then the cut is too short. For pants that are too long, take them to the tailor or your local dry cleaner, who can easily hem them. When you're purchasing jeans, ask the sales associate if the style comes in cuts like long, regular, or short (sometimes labeled as petite)—so that you can possibly save on the cost of tailoring.

Wear for the Weather

Style should also be functional. During a winter snowstorm, choose coats that can express shape, like an anorak style that will cinch at the waist, and retain a sense of your figure. While in the fall, a bright, printed scarf set against a neutral sweater will keep your neck warm, and provide a reminder of spring. Faux fur earmuffs are cozy and cute, but pull your hair back in a sleek bun or low ponytail for a grown-up take on the playful look. When you pick a hat, go for a style that doesn't match your scarf. (And beware: those hand-knit wool hat and scarf combos are dated—unless your grandma knitted you the pair, in which case you get a hall pass.)

CONCLUSION

It isn't what looks best on the hanger; it's what looks best on you. The fit of the outfit, the way the color looks against your skin, how the accessories complement your clothes, and the way your shoes balance out the overall look are all essential factors when it comes to fool-proof, confidence-boosting style. It's a long list of ingredients, but they're all worth considering. The rules and fashion mistakes discussed in this chapter will help narrow your focus and hone your critical eye when you're shopping for pieces or putting together a look. With fewer stumbling blocks in your way, you'll be able to start laying the foundation for years of great style.

 Fashion Action
Creating a Day-to-Night Outfit

Some of the best looks you can create are those that are appropriate for both lunch with friends *and* an evening dinner date. To pull off a seamless transition, start by wearing a solid base like a black shift dress or dark denim jeans with a royal purple knit tee. These are items that won't turn heads on their own but will provide a nice, solid style foundation for your complete day or evening look. Then, your simple additions to the outfit—such as the outerwear, shoes, purse, and jewelry—are the items that will transform the outfit from day to night. By keeping the base of the outfit the same for day and night, you won't have to find a spot to change, and the additional pieces will be small enough to fit in your car trunk or under your desk at work.

To complete this Fashion Action, practice creating your own transitional look. First, choose an item in your wardrobe that will act as your base. If possible, stick with solid colors, as prints are harder to transition away from. Next, pick accent pieces from the day and night columns below. Wear the day items, and place the night items in a backpack for later.

DAY

Shoe: Neutral colored pump or flat

Outerwear: Navy blazer, plaid trench coat, wool pea coat, faux fur–trimmed anorak

Jewelry: Wood bracelet, silver chain necklace, stud earrings

Handbag: Two-tone leather shoulder bag, canvas tote, nylon messenger

NIGHT

Shoe: Brightly colored heel, black patent leather flats, boots

Outerwear: Sequined cardigan, black sateen trench, leopard trimmed coat

Jewelry: Chunky cocktail ring, thick metal cuffs, rhinestone bangle bracelets, beaded chandelier earrings

Handbag: Chain-trimmed clutch, faux python foldover, metallic leather top-handle purse

CHAPTER 8

Styling Others

Once you've figured out how to style yourself, how about using some of your newfound skills on your fashion-challenged loved ones? Maybe your younger brother needs a new style before he starts high school, or maybe your best friend wants help putting together the perfect look for her first big date. I bet your mom could use a wardrobe update, too.

Styling others is a great way to not only improve your own styling abilities, but also to prepare for a potential career. But it all starts with that first client.

If you're going to help someone else create his or her perfect look, you'll need to treat the assignment like a real job, and treat the person you're styling like a client. You have to show complete professionalism the entire time, so no showing up late or taking phone calls while you're on the job. Style is a very personal art, and just like before, when you had to think about what your body shape was and who you wanted to look like before carving out your own fashion identity, now you have to help your client figure out what his or her own fashion ambitions are before you can help that person achieve them.

COMMUNICATE WITH YOUR CLIENT

The best way to start, of course, is with a few good questions. But in addition to your client's answers, you'll also need to keep an ear (and an eye) out for the styling ambitions that he or she may not be aware of yet. People rarely know what they want, and even when they do, they have a funny way of changing their minds—so the stylist's work is never really done.

The style journey is like a roller coaster, with lots of ups and downs and lots of ruts in between. Not wanting to deal, some people just get off the ride. They stop paying attention to what they're wearing, or hide in baggy clothes they believe are just too comfortable to part with. As a stylist, it's often your job to

Style Icon: Nicola Formichetti
Called "Mr. Gaga" by the *New York Times*, super stylist Nicola Formichetti is known for his bold, creative style (remember that meat dress!?), and for his list of clients, one of which is highlighted by his namesake: Lady Gaga. He first met her at a photo shoot for *V Magazine*, and now, along with creating out-of-this-world looks for Gaga, he's brought his style to a pop-up shop in New York City. The hand-picked items on display change daily, but in general they veer toward vintage Versace pieces, towering heels, and studded, red leather vests. He also applies his creative vision toward magazines like *Dazed and Confused* and *Vogue Hommes Japan*.

help change that perception. To do that, you have to be a great communicator, and assess your clients' needs along with their willingness to put in work on their own.

Some clients may be overwhelmed by the sheer amount of choices they have. Other clients may tell you they just don't know what looks best on their body. But whatever the case, once you know their reasons for wanting help, you can develop a clear plan to set reasonable expectations and then (hopefully) exceed those goals. That way, before your client starts fantasizing about becoming the next Gisele Bündchen, you can snap them back to reality and give examples of what style really *can* achieve: Confidence, a way to bring out natural beauty, and the opportunity to embrace (and show off!) body shape.

For friends, family, and other clients who *are* excited about fashion, you may not have to worry as much about scaling back your plans based on their level of skepticism, but you will need to pay close attention to the other aspects of their lives—such as their workload, their budget, and their attention to detail.

Check Your Ego at the Boutique Door

After coming this far, you're probably feeling pretty self-assured about your styling skills. You're confident, and feel secure in your own sense of style. Now hold on to all that confidence, courage, and security because there will always be a stylist who is better and more successful than you. There will always be clients who hate the looks you've spent hours creating for them. And there will always be salespeople who will unknowingly (let's hope) reject your sense of style, right in front of your client.

The best way to avoid crumbling at any of these scenarios is to check your ego at the boutique door. If a client doesn't agree with the rocking royal purple shift dress you chose for her, ask her why. She may hate everything about it, but on the other hand, maybe she's just averse to the color (easy fix, there are lots of other choices), or maybe she doesn't want to show off her legs (not a problem: purple pants are *au courant*, too!). If you're on a shopping trip with a client and a salesperson is continually stepping on your toes, wrap up your session at that store and head to the next one on the list—yep, it's that easy. You can't fully commit to helping your client if you're paying more attention to the way people are reacting to you.

HOW TO BE A GOOD INFLUENCE

As a stylist you're likely to have a big influence on what your client wears. (That's the idea, anyway.) However, be careful about how much influencing you actually do. Be sure to leave enough room for clients to still have fun with fashion, experiment on their own, and develop their own sense of style—just like you were able to do throughout this book.

As the stylist, you're really there to provide the courage to try a new style, or wear a new color, or shop in a store that he or she's been too intimidated to set foot in before. As you know, everything you wear says something about who you are or who you want to be. Keep that in mind when you're working with your clients. The outfits they wear should look tailor-made for them, not you.

STYLING SERVICES: A MENU

Once you know a bit more about your new clients and what they want from you, you can then decide together which of your services will work best for their needs. Most personal stylists have a basic service list that outlines every possible thing they can do for a client; we've included a similar list below. But remember, you don't have to accomplish everything on this list or do everything at once. It's all based on what your client wants to achieve and how much time you have.

Crash Course

A crash course in style is basically a one-day shopping trip with a client. You'll pick the stores (this will help streamline the experience for the client) and take your client on an adventure identifying the colors, fits, and styles that work with his or her body shape and taste. Now, not even a superhero stylist can create the perfect wardrobe in one day, but you can make good headway in creating additional looks for the client, or choosing key pieces to supplement his or her collection. And if your client is a friend who's short on money, just be sure to take pictures of everything that works, so that he or she can try and recreate those outfits when she's a little more flush.

➡ **Time Investment:** Eight hours.

Client Questionnaire

Before you start styling, have your friends or family members (aka you clients) fill out a questionnaire. This introductory set of questions is intended to help you find out exactly what your clients want to achieve with their new look. It provides basic information about the person's shoe size, waist measurement, and dress size, along with some more general information about their goals and what types of looks they're already wearing. A sample professional styling questionnaire is below, but you should feel free to expand the survey with any other questions that you think will help in determining what your client wants from you and their new style.

CLIENT NAME:

- How many nights per week do you need "going out" clothes?

- Describe what you wear for "going out":

- How many days per week do you wear jeans?

- If you had your choice, would you wear a dress or go for the "jeans and a cute top" look for a nice dinner out?

- Describe your typical work outfit:

- Describe what you wear to the gym:

- How many pairs of heels do you own?

- How many pairs of sneakers do you own?

- How many nice flat shoes do you own?

- How many pairs of boots do you own?

- What are your top three goals you want to get accomplished by using my services?

- What color dominates your wardrobe?

- Do you prefer loose or body hugging clothes?

- Is there anything that you absolutely won't wear?

- Who are your fashion icons?

- Do you like to be noticed in a crowd?

- What's the one piece of jewelry you couldn't live without?

- What is the ideal amount of time you would like to spend getting ready in the morning?

Seasonal Shopping

It's hard to believe but some people just don't like shopping and others just don't have the time for it. Both of these types of people are still known to hire stylists to shop for them—working within a budget to create new looks for each season. Unlike the crash course, where you take the client with you and explain the finer points of styling to them (don't forget about the sale rack!), with seasonal shopping you'll be working for the client on a predetermined basis, generally two or four times per year, to refill his or her wardrobe and stock up on essentials.

➡ **Time Investment:** Eight hours a day, several times a year.

Event Styling

Finding just the right outfit for a big event can be pretty stressful. It's like going to the grocery store when you're starving—which typically also results in a cart full of chocolate Ding Dongs and cream puffs instead of a real dinner. This is why many people enlist the help of a stylist just for special events. For this type of gig, you'll need to find out just how casual or dressy the event is, and from there, the client can go with you to various stores to try on the looks you've already determined to be a good match (these are items you've picked out at the stores and placed on hold for your client to see).

Time Investment: 12 hours—one full day to prequalify looks and one half day for the client to choose the best.

Closet Revamp and Style Audit

The easiest way for clients to revitalize their sense of style on the cheap is to go back to the clothes that they already have in their closet. For some people, all it takes is a new perspective (provided by you) to realize just how great their wardrobe really is. You'll go through the same process you undertook while curating your own closet in Chapter 5, but this time you'll provide the service to your client. Help your client choose which items to keep, which items to give away, and which items work best together.

➡ **Time Investment:** Depending on the size of the wardrobe, five to eight hours.

Look Book

When you've left your client's side and the brain fog starts to take over, it's nice for your client to have images of everything, for future reference. These images can be created for your client in what's called a look book. This is a personal stylebook with images of the client in some of the various outfits you've created together. The images don't have to be professional quality; you can even use your phone camera to capture the looks. Place the images in a Word doc of PDF. Your client can reference it on the computer or print it out.

➡ **Time Investment:** Five hours.

STYLING SUCCESS

When you start out with styling others, focus on the small victories first—like the feeling you get when you help your friend look her very best for a big event. Helping others shine in their newfound personal style, seeing the training wheels come off, and watching clients embrace their new wardrobe (while feeling fabulous the entire time) is one of the best feelings in the world. And if you find yourself with a true desire to change the way others feel about themselves—by inspiring their style—you may just want to turn a casual styling job here and there into a full-time career. And if you don't envision yourself ever wanting to dress a celebrity for the Oscars or a boy band for the Grammys, don't worry, because you can be a very successful stylist without celebrity clients.

➡ *Fashion Action*
Interview a Stylist

Still have questions about styling? Interview a stylist. Sure, it depends on a total stranger's cooperation, but you'd be surprised at just how receptive stylists are to meeting with young fashionistas about their career ambitions. Remember, professional stylists were once just like you, and started out with few (if any) clients. Reach out to styling agencies, local personal stylists (recommended by family and friends), and magazines in your city, and ask for an informational interview. Tell them you're considering a career in fashion or just want to learn more about the job, and that you'd love to sit down for a quick chat to find out more. Then, once they've agreed, follow these tips to get the most out of your interview.

1. Be prepared for the interview. This isn't just an opportunity to get your styling questions answered, it's also a chance for the stylist to learn more about you (which could turn in to a future assisting job or resource for your own styling gigs). Check the stylist's Twitter account, Facebook page, and personal website to find out more about him or her.

2. Craft questions you really want the answers to (and write them down). Don't waste the stylist's (or your) time by asking questions you don't really care about. If you're more interested in the stylist's career path (do you really need an internship?), stick to questions that reflect that fact. If you're curious where inspiration comes from (is a mood board useful?), ask that, too.

3. Meet in person. In the digital age it's tempting to do your interview through email, but meeting in person is the best way to get real (think: unedited) answers to your questions. You'll also get to wow the stylist with your personal style.

4. Don't lag on the follow-up. Send a thank you note within 24 hours of meeting with the stylist, and when you're ready, don't be afraid to inquire about assisting or internship possibilities (more about that in Chapter 9).

Styling as a Career

If you're great at multitasking, love being creative, and thrive in a fast-paced environment, then a career in the styling industry could be the prefect fit for you. There are many different types of stylists, but in each role there is one common denominator—you'll be part of a team. Whether it's just you and the client, or you, a photographer, editor, model, and team of assistants, the goal is to translate everything you've learned about fit, color, fabric, style, and body shape into a look that leaves the client feeling confident and beautiful.

TYPES OF STYLING

As a career, styling is really an umbrella term for many different types of jobs—each with its own perks. Not every type of styling job may be right for you, and that's okay. For example, do you like setting your own working hours like a personal stylist, or do you thrive in the 9–5 boundaries of in-house editorial styling? Are bigger (albeit more sporadic) paychecks—the kind often associated with fashion-show stylists—more important to you than the smaller but more regular payments you can earn as a wardrobe stylist? Contemplate each of the styling careers below and see where you'd fit best.

Editorial Styling

When your favorite fashion magazine showcases pages of models in elaborate photo shoots, the person responsible for pulling all of the clothing, accessories, and other elements together is an editorial stylist. Big magazines like *Teen Vogue*, *Vogue*, and *Glamour* often have an entire team of stylists working for them. Editorial stylists have to take all the inspiration that they find in street fashion, on the runways, in films, and even in other magazines, and then boil all of that information down to the very best looks that readers will want to recreate.

What the Work is Really Like: Typically, editorial stylists will spend their day prepping for and carrying out photo shoots. For each photo shoot, stylists will either work alone or with editors at the magazine to create the storyline (in fashion speak it's called "the concept") of the shoot. Once they have the concept down, stylists will then borrow all the necessary clothing and accessories directly from designers—often straight off the runway. Some editorial stylists will also be responsible for hiring the models and the photographer. If they need to hire the models, stylists will call for portfolios from modeling agencies and sift through each one to choose the right model. Then, with the team assembled, the real styling begins.

At the photo shoot, the stylist is on set prepping and styling the clothing to make sure it looks great on the model. As the pictures are being taken, the stylist is carefully analyzing each look, making sure there aren't any hanging threads and that the pins used to nip and tuck the garment aren't being seen on camera. When the photo shoot is done the editorial stylist may also work with the art director and the photographer to choose the best images for the magazine.

Which Personality Types Do It Best: At a magazine, an in-house stylist (meaning someone who gets a steady paycheck from the magazine) may have a professional title like fashion editor, associate fashion editor, assistant fashion editor, accessories editor, or the like. However, magazines can also hire freelance stylists that either work for themselves or for an agency. A freelance stylist will be hired on a per-shoot basis, with no promises of getting to style any additional shoots, so he or she needs to be able to work well without a lot of job security.

Fashion Show Stylist

There are fashion shows held all around the world, but the biggest ones are typically in New York, London, Milan, Paris, and Los Angeles. In-demand fashion show stylists will travel with the designer to ensure the collection shown on the runway (which generates lots of media buzz and sales for the designer) fully captures the designer's vision.

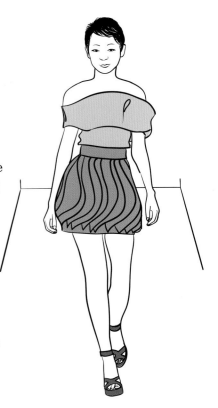

What the Work Is Really Like: Fashion shows often only last for a few minutes, but still take countless hours of preparation. Before the lights go on, stylists have to work with the designer to help edit all the clothing in the collection down into the few special looks that will be shown on the runway. Then stylists have to make sure that the looks will be ready in time (as production can fall behind), help hire the models, and then actually style the clothing throughout the big event. In a single fashion show there may be 30 different models to style. The stylist will work with assistants to get each model prepped to take the catwalk and determine the order in which the clothing will be shown on the runway.

Which Personality Types Do It Best: Fashion show stylists have to be quick on their feet. Juggling multiple models with quick clothing changes and one-of-a-kind garments makes organization and keeping cool under pressure key traits in this job role. For the biggest designer names and fashion shows (those held during media-heavy fashion weeks), there are only a few positions available. However, smaller local fashion shows held at malls, boutiques, and charity functions are also opportunities for a budding fashion show stylist.

Personal Styling

When Rachel Zoe creates the perfect red carpet look for her clients (who include Demi Moore and Anne Hathaway), she's acting as their personal stylist, ensuring that they have the best outfit for their body shape and the occasion. But personal styling isn't just for celebrities. It's about creating a look for any client—from your best friend to your mom to you—that fits and flatters.

What the Work Is Really Like: More than any other stylist, personal stylists have to wear many hats. One day they'll be helping a client edit and organize a wardrobe (just like you did to your own wardrobe earlier in the book). Another day they could be searching high-end department stores and consignment shops for just the right designer gown (maybe something for a client to wear to the opening of a symphony). And a few times a year they may shop with clients to boost their seasonal wardrobes, picking out the best coats for winter and resort wear for a summer vacation. Unlike other stylists, the personal stylist also has to act as a kind of teacher, training clients to see and understand what goes best with their body shape, complexions, and personalities.

Which Personality Types Do It Best: Most personal stylists work for themselves, and as a result they have to have an entrepreneurial spirit.

Style Icons: Rachel Zoe

Headline grabbing personal stylist Rachel Zoe has a litany of A-list clients that she dresses for big awards shows, movie premieres, and photo shoots. More recently though, she's expanded her role and built her own fashion empire—with a little bit of marketing help from her own reality television show. The show details the ups and downs (and meltdowns) of a big-time celebrity stylist. Rachel, who started her career as a magazine fashion editor, has gotten rave reviews for transferring her signature boho-style into her own high-end fashion line.

Setting budgets and marketing their services are all part of the job. But aside from knowing how to be their own bosses, personal stylists also have to be able to work with different types of personalities, age groups, and body shapes. Not all of personal stylists' clients will be five-foot-ten, rail-thin model-types. They'll work with hourglass-shaped grandmas, inverted triangle college students, and rectangular mamas. Because personal stylists work directly with clients, they'll also get lots of one-on-one interaction. They'll be expected to give clients pointers on how to choose the right look for their own body type and spend long hours sifting through racks of clothing in order to pick out the few essential, indispensable items.

Wardrobe Styling

Just like the editorial stylist, who works to create the perfect image in print, the wardrobe stylist creates the best look for film and television. Think about it—every time you see an actor in a commercial, on your favorite sitcom, or in a movie, that person's look had to be chosen and put together by someone, and that someone is the wardrobe stylist. Because wardrobe stylists dress each character in a storyline, they need to have (or gain) experience styling all sizes, shapes, and ages (which can be more interesting than styling the same model types each day). Most wardrobe stylists live in the Los Angeles area—where many television shows and movies are filmed—but travel is often required when filming is done on location. Wardrobe stylist positions for commercials or movies tend to be very temporary positions; they only last for as long as filming goes on, which is often just a day, and rarely extends beyond a few months. Wardrobe styling gigs for television shows are more long-term (well, unless the show gets cancelled) and tend to have set hours (since television shows usually tape each week for the entire season).

What the Work Is Really Like: A typical day as a wardrobe stylist will be spent working long hours on set. You (and if you're lucky and well-established, your team of assistants) will have to prepare all the clothing for the day's shoot, fit each actor, and then stick around to make sure that each piece looks its best.

Which Personality Types Do It Best: Like most people in the entertainment industry, you've got to be tenacious and willing to start at the very bottom to succeed. If your parents haven't won an Emmy, and

The 1990s

Style Through the Decades

Shows like *Saved by the Bell, Beverly Hills, 90210* (the original), and *Clarissa Explains It All* dominated television and '90s teen style. Teens everywhere were rocking scrunchies, overalls, crop tops, floral prints, and high-waisted acid-washed denim jeans. And although the decade is now long gone, it hasn't been forgotten—Justin Bieber has even paid homage to TV character and teen style icon Kelly Kapowski (played by Tiffani-Amber Thiessen on *Saved by the Bell*) with a shirt emblazoned with her picture (in all her '90s fashion glory) that he wore at a red carpet event.

if you don't have a single connection in Hollywood, you'll want to start by getting a few years of experience either by assisting other stylists, or by getting a college degree in fashion (or taking classes in fashion styling). Once you've built solid experience, your goal should be to get an agent who will help you book wardrobe styling jobs (and who can be especially helpful in getting you work on commercials, which come up more frequently than television shows or films). Beginning wardrobe stylists can also work their way up the styling ladder by offering their services on student films and low-budget independent films.

Catalog Styling

Catalog stylists have a challenging job. They need to create a nice fit, choose the perfect color combinations, and pair the right prints together to create a look that will succeed in selling an outfit. Unlike the editorial stylist, who has endless options for creating the perfect look, the catalog stylist can't supplement clothing with items that the catalog doesn't sell. For example, if the catalog is only selling two pairs of shoes in a given season, the catalog stylist may have to make those exact pairs work in every single look. This is why catalog stylists are the puzzle masters of the fashion styling world. They have a set number of puzzle pieces (clothing items and accessories) and must use each item to create various looks for an entire catalog.

What the Work Is Really Like: Working within these restrictions, the typical day of a catalog stylist can be like putting together one of those 1,000 piece jigsaw puzzles—you know you can only use the provided pieces, but if you just had a few more corner options it would really help...But that puzzle master mentality will also really help to hone the catalog stylist's skills. If a piece of clothing is presenting some difficulty (perhaps it doesn't look great on the model, or maybe the color isn't right with the accessories), catalog stylists don't have the option of using a different look and instead, they'll have to use their styling fairy godmother skills to make it work.

Which Personality Types Do It Best: A fashion company may only produce one catalog per season, which means most catalog stylists are freelancers or are hired through a styling agency. However, with the advent of online shopping, there are more opportunities for internet catalog stylists who need to be available to constantly update the site for returning customers. There are also some stylists who work in a sort of hybrid role for department stores that have online shopping sites to supplement their print catalogs. Whatever capacity catalog stylists work in, there is one trait they share; they are very detail oriented.

GETTING YOUR FOOT IN THE DOOR

Whichever segment of the styling industry you decide to dig your heels into, you're sure to run into a lot of competition. There are entire college majors dedicated to individual facets of the fashion industry and a ton of talented people just waiting for their big break. In addition to a solid education, the best way to get your foot in the door is with some real-world experience—and with the right attitude, real-world experience is definitely something you can find.

Independent Stylist

As an assistant to a professional stylist you'll have an insider's view of the blood, sweat, and tears (literally) that go into every serious fashion project. The job isn't glamorous, and you may do more schlepping than actual styling, but the contacts you'll make will be priceless.

How to Get the Job: Reach out to local agencies that represent stylists, and offer your services as an assistant. Make sure they know that you're willing to work long hours for little pay. This isn't a get-rich-quick job, and you'll have to prove your styling skills and get some clients of your own before you can earn enough money to buy a single pair of Louboutins.

The Good and the Bad: Working for a professional stylist will provide you with a built-in clientele on which to practice your styling skills.

When it's time to leave the nest and start your own styling business, be professional and don't poach clients from your former employer (the fashion industry is small, so staying on good terms with past bosses is important). It's also important to have patience. Making the transition from assistant to fashion powerhouse isn't always quick. For three years Britt Bardo assisted well-known stylist Andrea Lieberman. The experience gave her the edge she needed to go out on her own with her first celeb client, Jennifer Lopez. Since then, Britt has worked with Kate Hudson, Eva Mendes, and Cameron Diaz and is the style expert for a big-name cosmetics company; recently, Britt has teamed up with another stylist to start the clothing line ROSE.

> ### The 2000s
> ## Style Through the Decades
> The 2000s were marked by an attraction to accessible designer fashions. Target's Go International Collection was launched and featured reasonably priced, limited edition collections by high-end designers like Rodarte, Proenza Schouler, Zac Posen, and Erin Fetherston. H&M scored a high-low collaboration with Chanel's Karl Lagerfeld and Versace. Payless unveiled wallet-friendly shoe collections designed by names like *Project Runway*'s Christian Siriano, and Giambattista Valli created the lower priced Impulse line for Macy's.

Magazines

As in most other industries today, an internship is a key way to get your stiletto in the door, but in the super small world of fashion magazines it's even more important than usual.

How to Get the Job: Almost all magazines have a fashion or photo department. Reach out to them to inquire about a styling internship. Check on the magazine's website to see if it has a formal internship program, too (since if this is the case, you may even get school credit).

The Good and the Bad: At a magazine, you'll be exposed to photo shoots, and, if you're lucky, you may even get to assist the fashion editor on styling a fashion spread, which can provide some impressive images for your portfolio. However, don't assume that assisting at a photo shoot will mean that you'll be doing anything creative. Chances are, you'll just be steaming clothing and boxing up the wardrobe after the shoot. But we all have to start somewhere!

Boutiques

Working at a boutique is a great way to stay on top of new trends and see what types of looks your customers (aka your future clients!) are gravitating toward. Plus, working at a boutique doesn't have to be a full-time position, so if you're still in school or already have a job, don't exclude yourself. You can work one day a week during the summer, or even a few hours after class during the school year.

How to Get the Job: If you don't have enough experience to get hired as an official employee, offer your help as an intern at your favorite local boutique. Ask the manager or the owner about interning as a window stylist. In this role you'll help to dress the mannequins, and not only will you get some much needed styling experience, you'll also get exposure to seasonal trends.

The Good and the Bad: At a boutique you'll have important face-to-face interactions with people who have money to spend on clothing—and who just may need the services of an up-and-coming professional stylist like you. Unfortunately, in the meantime, boutiques aren't known for paying their employees very well.

Agencies

Many traditional modeling agencies now represent stylists, as well. An internship with an agency will give you some key insights into what the agency looks for in recruiting new talent, how jobs are booked, and how the agency gains new clients for its talent.

How to Get the Job: Call styling agencies in your area and ask for an informational interview. This is when you can bring your portfolio (more about that later in this chapter) and inquire about internship opportunities.

The Good and the Bad: The best part about interning with a styling agency is the opportunity to fill in for the professional stylists at photo shoots (because everyone has to take a day off eventually) and assist stylists on shoots. However, as with any assistant role, the amount of styling you'll actually get to do will depend on the person you're working for, and in most cases you'll be relegated to way-behind-the-camera work like running errands, pressing garments, and standing in line at the post office.

Photographers

Fashion photographers, wedding photographers, and everyday portrait photographers all have one thing in common: They can benefit from the help of a stylist. Their clients want to look their best on camera—and that's where you come in, making sure the wardrobe selection is just right.

How to Get the Job: Photographers aren't necessarily posting job openings for styling help. It's a position you may have to help create. As with any job, be clear about what you're asking for and seek out reputable photographers (ask for recommendations from family and friends).

The Good and the Bad: Working with a photographer will give you experience working on photo shoots (which will provide lots of photos for your portfolio), but your schedule will be dictated by the photographer (who will be setting up the shoots with clients)—which means the hours could be less than ideal.

CREATING A PORTFOLIO

If you've ever applied for a job, you've probably had to fill out an application or even supply your résumé, which gives the prospective employer a basic sense of your skills and work experience. A portfolio offers this same kind of information, except it provides it in a completely visual way. If you don't have a portfolio, follow these steps to create your own.

Step 1: Compile Your Work

Use the photographs you'll take in the Fashion Action photo shoot (at the end of this chapter) as the basic material for your portfolio. If you've assisted on any other photo shoots, then include those images in your pile, too.

Step 2: Edit, Edit, and Then Edit Some More

You'll need to be a strong editor to choose just three images, out of all your options, to include in the final portfolio. You can add more later, but three is a good number to start out with. This follows the "odd rule" of composition. Groupings of three, five, or seven images tend to give the portfolio a nice balance and will also create the illusion of having more images in your portfolio than you really have.

Step 3: Put it All Together

Create a cover page with your name and contact information, and then organize the rest of the document with your images—preferably with one on each page. If you're creating a digital PDF copy of your portfolio (which is the cheapest way to do it), name your PDF something simple, like your full name. When you email your PDF to a potential internship employer, you'll want your name to be easily recognizable in the attachment. If you have an in-person interview, print out the PDF on thick resume paper, and if your budget allows for it, include the printout in a folder with clear protective page covers.

Style Icons: Tavi Gevinson

In the suburbs of Chicago, teenager Tavi Gevinson sits in her bedroom and types up her musings about fashion and life on her blog, Style Rookie. Tavi started blogging at 11, and in a few short years she's amassed style credentials that insiders four times her age are still reaching for. She has penned fashion articles for *Harper's Bazaar*, been the inspiration for Rodarte's fashion line for Target, sat front row at a Marc Jacobs fashion show, traveled to Paris to attend the couture shows, flown to Tokyo to be the guest of honor at the Comme des Garçons holiday party, and styled her first photo shoot for the uber-hip *BlackBook* magazine—all while still in high school.

➡ Fashion Action
Style your own fashion shoot!

It's a bit of a conundrum: If you don't have a styling job then you won't have pictures from past photo shoots to include in your portfolio—but often, you can only get the job if you've got the portfolio. Instead of trying to figure out that puzzle (yup, pretty much impossible), take charge of the situation and create your own images instead. Then, you can use those new photos in your portfolio and use your portfolio to try and land a gig.

To style your own fashion shoot, all you need to do is follow these simple steps.

1. **Get a model.** Ask a friend, a parent, or a sister or brother to act as your model. Analyze his or her body shape and refer to Chapter 4 to determine what type of clothing would look best on them.

2. **Decide on a photographer.** If you don't have a friend or family member who's a budding photographer, then just take the photos yourself, a la The Sartorialist.

3. **Create a concept.** This is the story your shoot will tell. Is it a look at fall fashion trends? A retrospective of '80s punk fashion? A prom style spread? It's up to you!

4. **Choose a location.** Your home or a friend's home is the easiest place to start, because you'll need to get permission from the land or homeowner to work anywhere else.

5. **Get the clothing.** Before you have your model "on set," you'll need to pull all the clothing you want to use in the shoot. Ask the model if you can pull clothing from his or her closet; this way you'll have the sizing right. If you need additional items, try thrift stores and your own closet to keep your costs low. Choose items from the closet that will work with your concept for the shoot. For example, if your story is about a girl away at summer camp, you probably won't need any sophisticated nighttime looks. Instead pull items you'd really bring to summer camp: jeans, tees, a bathing suit, the perfect hiking outfit, and the like.

6. **Prep your clothing.** No matter how great the outfit is, if wrinkles and creases are all you see, that's all the camera will see, too. Check each garment's "care-for" tag, and if it won't cause damage, then steam or iron it so it looks fresh and brand new.

7. **Create the looks.** Once you have your model and the clothes on set, it's time to have the model actually try on the looks. For a full-day shoot, try and put together eight looks that you really love. For a half-day shoot, four is ideal. Organize each look (along with the relevant accessories) according to the order in which it will be shot.

8. **Style the model.** Although you've already chosen the looks, you'll still need to be available to fix and perfect each outfit. Bring the stylist kit you created in Chapter 3 to pin back any loose garments or shorten a skirt on the fly.

9. **Take the photos.** And have fun!

Somer Flaherty is a California-based fashion stylist with more than a decade of experience in the fashion industry. She is a graduate of the journalism program at San Francisco State University, and is currently also a journalism instructor at the Academy of Art University. Her work has appeared in numerous magazines, advertising campaigns, and catalogues (not to mention the wardrobes of private clients throughout the country).

To Mom, for your never ending encouragement and always providing a pen and paper throughout my childhood.

To Dad, who knew absolutely nothing about fashion but had invaluable confidence in all my projects.

To Sam Tejwani, for putting up with the long, long hours and always having an honest opinion about my outfits.

To Nikki Wood, for giving me my first paying job in styling and Mimi Towle for encouraging me to write about it.

To Danielle Goodman, for the greatest early morning fashion brainstorming sessions in the world!

To the best girl friends in the world (you know who you are), for providing me with tireless support and fashion inspiration each day.

To Emily Glaubinger, for putting all those images in my head on paper and creating amazing artwork.

To Hallie Warshaw, for being the first person to get behind this book. Without you it wouldn't have ever seen the light of day! And to the rest of the team at Zest, including my editor extraordinaire Dan Harmon for getting me to the finish line.

Thank you.

SCHOOL LIFE

97 Things to Do Before You Finish High School
by Steven Jenkins & Erika Stalder

Been There, Survived That
Getting Through Freshman Year of High School
edited by Karen Macklin

Crap
How to Deal With Annoying Teachers, Bosses, Backstabbers, and Other Stuff that Stinks
by Erin Elisabeth Conley, Karen Macklin, & Jake Miller

The Dictionary of High School B.S.
From Acne to Varsity, All the Funny, Lame, and Annoying Aspects of High School Life
by Lois Beckwith

Freshman
Tales of 9th Grade Obsessions, Revelations, and Other Nonsense
by Corinne Mucha

Take Me With You
Off-to-College Advice From One Chick to Another
by Nikki Roddy

Uncool
A Girl's Guide to Misfitting In
by Erin Elisabeth Conley

DATING + RELATIONSHIPS

Crush
A Girl's Guide to Being Crazy in Love
by Erin Elisabeth Conley

The Date Book
A Girl's Guide to Going Out With Someone New
by Erika Stalder

Dumped
A Girl's Guide to Happiness After Heartbreak
by Erin Elisabeth Conley

Girls Against Girls
Why We Are Mean to Each Other, and How We Can Change
by Bonnie Burton

Kiss
A Girl's Guide to Puckering Up
by Erin Elisabeth Conley

The Mother Daughter Cookbook
Recipes to Nourish Relationships
by Lynette Rohrer Shirk

Queer
The Ultimate LGBT Guide for Teens
by Kathy Belge & Marke Bieschke

Split In Two
Keeping It Together When Your Parents Live Apart
by Karen Buscemi

HEALTH 101

Girl in a Funk
Quick Stress Busters (and Why They Work)
by Tanya Napier & Jenn Kollmer

Sex: A Book for Teens
An Uncensored Guide to Your Body, Sex, and Safety
by Nikol Hasler

Skin
The Bare Facts
by Lori Bergamotto

STYLE

Fashion 101
A Crash Course in Clothing
by Erika Stalder

The Look Book
50 Iconic Beauties and How to Achieve Their Signature Styles
by Erika Stalder

POP CULTURE

Dead Strange
The Bizarre Truths Behind 50 World-Famous Mysteries
by Matt Lamy

The End
50 Apocalyptic Visions From Pop Culture
That You Should Know About...before it's too late
by Laura Barcella

How to Fight, Lie, and Cry Your Way to Popularity (and a prom date)
Lousy Life Lessons from 50 Teen Movies
by Nikki Roddy

Reel Culture
50 Classic Movies You Should Know About
(So You Can Impress Your Friends)
by Mimi O'Connor

Scandalous!
50 Shocking Events You Should Know About
(So You Can Impress Your Friends)
by Hallie Fryd